Ordeal by Labyrinth

Mircea Eliade

The University of Chicago Press
Chicago · London

Ordeal by Labyrinth

CONVERSATIONS · WITH · CLAUDE-HENRI · ROCQUET

Translated by
Derek Coltman

With the essay
"Brancusi and Mythology"

MIRCEA ELIADE is the Sewell L. Avery Distinguished
Service Professor in the Divinity School and Professor
in the Committee on Social Thought of the University of Chicago.

The University of Chicago Press, Chicago 60637
The University of Chicago Press, Ltd., London

Originally published in French under the title
*L'Épreuve du Labyrinthe: Entretiens avec Claude-Henri
Rocquet.* Copyright © 1978 by Pierre Belfond, Paris.

Library of Congress Cataloging in Publication Data

Eliade, Mircea, 1907–
   Ordeal by labyrinth.

   Translation of L'Épreuve du labyrinthe.
   Bibliography: p.
   1. Eliade, Mircea, 1907–   . 2. Religion
historians—United States—Biography.   3. Religion—
Study and teaching.   I. Rocquet, Claude-Henri.
II. Title.
BL43.E4A3213   291'.092'4 [B]   81-21796
ISBN 0-226-20387-5   AACR2

✑ Contents

Preface

This book's title makes its nature clear enough: *Ordeal by Labyrinth*. Custom suggests that the confidant should provide a preface to the dialogue his questions have elicited. I can at least give the reasons that led me to approach the frontiers of that almost legendary region, Mircea Eliade, in order to question him. It was because, when I was twenty and read my first book by Eliade—I think it was *Images and Symbols*—in the library of the Institut d'Etudes Politiques (where, to tell the truth, I had scarcely any right to be), the things I found there—the archetypes, the magic, the links between things, the myths of the pearl and the shell, baptisms and floods—all affected me more immediately and more deeply than the teachings of my political economy teachers: Eliade was imparting the very taste and meaning of things. And it was because, years later, given the task of making budding architects understand that human space cannot be truly measured unless it is oriented in accordance with the cardinal points of the human heart, I had no better allies than the Bachelard of *La Poétique de l'espace* and the Eliade of *The Sacred and the Profane*. Last, it is because, reading and rereading his *Journal,* wandering through that world much as one strolls through Venice or Siena, enjoying the presence of the man, following the long path of his life, I suddenly glimpsed, gleaming, very close, through the edifice of all his books, an individual flame. I think my desire has been fulfilled: I have met the mythic ancestor, I can say that we have become friends; and through my persistence

I have brought into being at the center of Eliade's work—that rich territory of writings and thought—the microcosm and crossroads, as it were, of these *Conversations*.

To penetrate the labyrinth of a work and a life, in order to seek out its unity, any entrance will do. The apprenticeship in India at twenty and the closeness to Jung at Eranos conferences twenty years later; the profound Romanian roots, recognizable even in his way of accepting the world as his homeland; the long list of myths compiled and also profoundly understood; the work of the historian and the primitive passion for inventing fables; Nicolas de Cusa and the Himalayas: it is clear why the theme of the *coincidentia oppositorum* echoes so often and so clearly through Eliade's work. But ought we to say that in the end they all converge? Perhaps, rather, that everything sprang from the original soul and that the soul, like a seed, like a tree, drawing all the various aspects of the world toward it in order to answer the world by interrogating it, enriches the world by its presence. In the end, the origin is made manifest by everything that has evolved and been assembled since.

I went to meet a man whose work had lit up my adolescence, and I met a mind of here and now. Eliade has never made the mistake of wanting the social sciences to be modeled on the natural sciences; he has never forgotten that, to understand things of a human order, one must have understood them already and that the questioner can never claim to stand outside what he is questioning. He has never succumbed to the temptation of Freudianism, of Marxism, of structuralism—or, rather, to the temptation of that cocktail of dogma and fashion usually denoted by those terms. In short, he has never forgotten the irreducible role of interpretation, the inextinguishable desire for meaning, for philosophic discourse. It must be stressed, however, that this *topicality* of Eliade's is not that of the magazines. No one has thought of seeing him as the precursor of the California pilgrims to Katmandu; no one would dream of discovering him as some kind of unheralded "new philosopher." If Mircea Eliade is *modern,* it is because he grasped the fact, half a century ago now, that the "crisis of mankind" is in fact a crisis of Western man and that it would be wise to understand it, and survive it, by recognizing the archaic, "uncivilized," familiar roots of the human condition.

Mircea Eliade, "historian of religions . . ." This very official way of defining him entails the risk of misunderstanding him. When we say *history,* let us at least understand *memory* and then remember that all memory is a present, a *now.* Let us also remember that, for Eliade, the touchstone of the religious is the sacred, which is to say an encounter with or a presentiment of the *real,* and that this reality is the lodestone of art as well as of religion. But on what basis do we discriminate between them? I believe that we can grasp Eliade's thinking best if we perceive its relationship to Malraux's. If Malraux sees art as *the coinage of the absolute,* which is to say a form of the religious spirit, Eliade regards the rituals and myths of archaic man—his religion—as so many works of art or masterpieces. Both minds have this in common, however: both have recognized the ineradicable value of the imaginary, have seen that there is no means of knowing alien or deserted imaginary worlds other than by recreating them, presenting them as an offering to an unforeseeable humanity. Neither the passion for knowledge nor the attentiveness of the philosopher seems to be Eliade's essential home; rather, it is the wellspring of the poem, by means of which mortal life sometimes transfigures itself and overwhelms us with hope.

Claude-Henri Rocquet

Ordeal by Labyrinth

Origins and Their Meaning

Name and Origin

·R·   Mircea Eliade. That is a beautiful name.

·E·   Why do you say that? Eliade: *hēlios;* and Mircea: *mir,* the Slavic root meaning *peace* . . .

·R·   . . . and world?

·E·   And world too, yes; or rather, cosmos.

·R·   I wasn't thinking primarily of the meaning but of the music.

·E·   The name Eliade is Greek in origin and probably goes back to *hēlios.* Earlier, it was written Heliade. There were puns on *hēlios* and *Hellade:* "sun" and "Greek." Only it wasn't my father's real name. My grandfather was called Jeremiah. But in Romania, when someone's a little bit lazy, or very slow or hesitant, people are always quoting the proverb: "Oh, you're like Jeremiah, who couldn't get his cart out." And they used to say it to my father when he was a schoolboy. So he decided that as soon as he came of age he'd change his name. He chose the name Eliade because it had belonged to a very famous nineteenth-century writer: Eliade Radulescu. So he became "Eliade." And I'm grateful to him, because I prefer it to Jeremiah. I like my name.

·R·   Those who have read your *Journal** already know something about what kind of man you are and the broad outlines of your life. But the *Journal* doesn't begin until 1945, when you were almost forty and living in Paris. Before that you had already lived in Romania, India, London, and Lisbon. You were a famous writer in Romania and an Orientalist. The *Journal* does contain allusions to those things, but we still know almost nothing about the years before your arrival in Paris and, in particular, about your childhood.

·E·   Well, I was born on the ninth of March 1907, a terrible month in Romanian history because it was the time of the peasant uprisings in all the provinces. In high school they always said to me: "Ah, you were born in the middle of the peasant revolt." My father was in the army, like his brother. He was a captain. In Bucharest I went to primary school on Mântuleasa Street, the school I decribed later in *Strada Mântuleasa* (*The Old Man and the Bureaucrats*). Then I attended the Spiru-Haret High School. Quite a good one it was, too. It was referred to as the Romanian Lycée Jules Ferry.

·R·   Your father was an army officer . . . But tell me some more about your family.

·E·   I think of myself as a synthesis: my father was a Moldavian, my mother was an Oltenian. In Romanian culture Moldavia represents the emotional side, melancholy, an interest in philosophy and poetry, and a certain passivity in the face of life. Moldavians are interested not so much in politics as in political programs and paper revolutions. I in-

---

**No Souvenirs: Journal, 1957–1969* (New York, 1975). The French edition (*Fragments d'un Journal*) begins with entries from the year 1945.

For convenience, the titles of Mr. Eliade's works will be rendered for the most part in English even when the works themselves have not yet been translated from the French or Romanian. For clarification, the reader is invited to consult the bibliography of Mr. Eliade's works at the back of the book.

herited that Moldavian tradition from my father and my grandfather, who was a peasant. I'm very proud of being able to say that I'm the third generation in our family to wear shoes. Because my great-grandfather went barefoot, or wore *opinci,* a sort of sandal. In winter I had a pair of enormous boots. It was a common Romanian expression: "second, third, or fourth shoe generation." I was third generation. And that Moldavian heritage is the origin of my tendency toward melancholy, poetry, metaphysics—let us say, toward "the night." My mother's family, on the other hand, came from Oltenia, which is the western province, bordering on Yugoslavia. Oltenians are ambitious, energetic folk, passionate about horses—and not just the peasants but the *haïduks,* too, the traders: they sell horses—sometimes they even steal them! It's the most energetic of the provinces, the most high-spirited, and you might even say the most brutal; it's the complete opposite of Moldavia. My parents met in Bucharest; and when I became conscious of my heritage, I was very happy about it. Like anybody, like all adolescents, I had fits of despair, of melancholy, sometimes almost amounting to real clinical depression. That was my Moldavian heritage. Yet, at the same time, I was aware of an enormous fund of energy inside me. I used to say to myself: that comes from my mother. I owe them both a great deal. At thirteen I was in the Scouts, and I was allowed to spend vacations in the mountains, the Carpathians, or boating on the Danube, in the delta, on the Black Sea. My family let me do anything. My mother especially. When I was twenty-one, I said to her: I'm going to India. Socially, we belonged to the petty bourgeoisie, the lower middle class, but my parents didn't turn a hair. This was in 1928, and some of even the greatest Sanskrit scholars in the West still had no firsthand knowledge of India. I believe Louis Renou was thirty-five by the time he made his first visit there. And I went when I was twenty. My family let me do whatever I wanted: visit Italy, buy all sorts of books, study Hebrew, Persian. I was given enormous freedom.

·R·   You say your family belonged to the petty

bourgeoisie; but they displayed a certain taste for things of the mind. Wouldn't it be more accurate to say that they belonged to the "cultured class"?

·E· Yes. They laid no claim to being highly cultured, but at the same time they didn't have that willfully closed mind one finds in many, yes, let's say petty-bourgeois families.

·R· You were an only child?

·E· No, there were three of us. My brother was born two years before me, and my sister four years after. It was a stroke of luck, coming between them like that. Because the favorite, needless to say, was for many years my brother, the oldest; and later it was my sister, the baby of the family. I can't say I didn't feel loved, but I was never suffocated by an excess of love by either my mother or my father. That was a great piece of luck. Plus the bonus of having a brother as a friend and, later on, my sister too.

·R· The picture you paint is of a man perfectly happy about both his birth and his origins.

·E· Yes, that's true. I can't remember ever criticizing my family or being rebellious as an adolescent. Yet I wasn't very well off, I didn't have much money to buy books with. My mother used to give me some occasionally out of what she'd saved from the housekeeping or when we sold something. Later on, we even rented part of our house. I didn't have a lot of money, but I never felt deprived. I was quite content with my place in society, with my family.

Dragon and Eden

·R· What images do you recall from your early childhood?

·E· The first image . . . I was two, two and a half. It was in a forest. I was there, looking. My mother was out of sight. We were on a picnic. I'd crawled a few yards, and I was lost. Then, quite suddenly, I saw a huge, resplendent blue lizard in front of me. It dazzled me. I wasn't afraid, but I was so spellbound by the beauty of it, that enormous blue creature. . . . I could feel my heart thumping, out of excitement and fear, yet at the same time I could see the fear in the lizard's eyes, too. I could see its heart beating. That image was with me for years.

Another time—at about the same age, I imagine, since I see myself still crawling—it was something at home. There was a room, a parlor I wasn't supposed to go into. In fact, I think it was always kept locked. One day, it was a summer afternoon, about four o'clock, and everyone was out—my father at the barracks, my mother visiting a neighbor—I crawled up to the door, I pushed, and the door opened. I went in, right inside. And what I found was for me an extraordinary experience: there were green curtains at the windows, and because it was summer they were drawn, so that the whole room was tinged with green. It was so odd, I felt I was inside a ripe green grape. I was fascinated by that green light, a golden green; I gazed around me, and it was truly a space I'd never known before, a quite different world. That was the only time. Next day I tried to open the door again, but it was already locked.

·R· Do you know why you weren't allowed into the room?

·E· Oh, there were shelves with a lot of knicknacks on them. But apart from that, my mother and some of the other townswomen were organizing a big children's party with a tombola, and the prizes were being stored in our parlor. My mother quite rightly didn't want her children to see such an enormous quantity of toys.

·R· Did you see them when you went in, the toys?

·E· Yes, but in any case I knew they were there; I'd seen my mother bringing them home. That wasn't what caught my eye. It was the color. It really was like being inside a grape. It was very hot weather, and the light was extraordinarily bright, but it was filtered through the curtains. The light was green. I really did feel that I was suddenly right inside a grape. Have you read my novel *The Forbidden Forest?* In that, Stéphane remembers a mysterious room from his childhood, the "Sambô" room. He wonders what the name meant. It is nostalgia for a space he'd once known, a space unlike any other room he's ever been in. Clearly, in my description of that "Sambô" room I was calling on my own experience: the extraordinary experience of entering a totally different space.

·R· Were you slightly alarmed at your own daring or merely wonderstruck?

·E· Wonderstruck.

·R· You weren't at all afraid? You didn't have the feeling that you were doing something delightfully wicked?

·E· No. What drew me in was the color, the calm, and the beauty of it: it was our parlor, with its pictures, its shelves of ornaments, but all green! Bathed in green light.

·R· Here I'd like to turn to Eliade the expert on myths, the hermeneut and friend of Jung. What does he think about these two incidents?

·E· Well, it's very odd, but it's never occurred to me to try to interpret them! For me they've always been just memories. But it's true that the meeting with the monster, that lizard with its startling, otherworldly beauty . . .

·R· With the dragon . . .

·E· Yes, it was the Dragon. But the female Dragon, the androgynous Dragon, because it really was so lovely! I was enthralled by its beauty, by that astounding blueness.

·R· Despite your own fear you were still sufficiently in command of yourself to sense the lizard's fear.

·E· I could see it! I could see the fear in its eyes, I could see it being afraid of the little child. That huge and very beautiful saurian monster was afraid of the child. I was thunderstruck by that.

·R· You said that the Dragon was extremely beautiful

because it was "female, androgynous." Does that mean that beauty, for you, is essentially linked with the feminine?

·E· No, I also perceive an androgynous beauty and a masculine beauty. I cannot reduce beauty, even that of the human body, to feminine beauty.

·R· Why do you talk of "androgynous beauty" in the case of the lizard?

·E· Because it was perfect. It was everything: grace and terror, ferocity and smile, everything was there.

·R· The word "androgynous" is not without its importance in your work. You have written at length on the subject of the androgyne.

·E· But never without stressing the point that the *androgyne* and the *hermaphrodite* are not the same thing. In the hermaphrodite the two sexes coexist. You find statues of men with breasts. Whereas the androgyne represents the ideal of perfection: the two sexes are fused. It is another human species, a different species. And that is important, I think. Of course they both—the hermaphrodite as well as the androgyne—exist in world culture, not just that of Europe. I personally am attracted by the androgyne. I see it as possessing a perfection that is difficult to attain, is perhaps never attained, in either sex separately.

·R· That makes me think of a certain opposition to be found in "structural" analysis between the bestial and the divine in archaic Greece. Would you say that the hermaphrodite belongs on the side of the monster and the androgyne on that of the god?

·E· No, because I don't believe that the hermaphrodite represents a monstrous form. It is a desperate effort to achieve totalization. But it isn't a fusion, it isn't a unity.

·R· And what meaning do you attribute to the room-inside-a-grape? Do you know why that memory has remained so vivid?

·E· What impressed me was the atmosphere, an

9

atmosphere of paradise—that green, that golden green. And then the calm in there, the absolute calm. And I penetrated that zone, that sacred space. I say "sacred," because this particular space was wholly "other" in its quality; it was not profane, not of the everyday world. It was not part of the ordinary world I lived in with my father, my mother, my brother, the yard, the house. No, it was something quite other. A heavenly thing. A forbidden place before, and again afterwards. In my memory it remains something truly exceptional. I called it "paradisal" later on, when I'd learned the word. It wasn't a religious experience, but I understood that I was now in a quite different space and that I was experiencing something completely new. The proof is the way that memory has haunted me.

·R· A *totally different* space of greenery, or greenness, and of gold; a sacred, forbidden place (yet entered without transgression, it seems)—those are truly images of paradise: green, the original green; gold; the sphericity of the place; that light. Yes, as though in your earliest childhood you had lived for a moment in heaven. Or shall we say in paradise, in Eden, the original paradise?

·E· That's it, yes.

·R· But, echoing behind your "wholly other," I can obviously hear, as you yourself can, the words that Rudolf Otto uses to define the sacred: *ganz andere.* And I can see, too, that this childhood image is akin to those that fascinated and enthralled you as an adult, when you encountered them in myths. Anyone who has read your books, hearing of that memory without knowing it was yours, would probably still think of you. Who knows, perhaps these two crucial experiences—your meeting with the dragon and that closed, luminous, paradisal room—profoundly affected the direction of your life.

·E· Yes, perhaps. Who knows? Consciously, I know what books, which discoveries during my adolescence, awakened my interest in religions and myths. But I have no way of telling how far those childhood experiences determined my life.

·R· Hieronymus Bosch, in his *Garden of Delights,* depicts beings living inside fruits.

·E· I didn't feel that I was really inside an enormous fruit. It was just that I couldn't compare that green-golden light to anything but being enclosed inside a grape. So it wasn't the idea of the fruit, of *living inside a fruit,* but that of finding myself inside a certain space—a paradisal space. It was the experience of a certain light.

How I Discovered the Philosopher's Stone

·R· Your first school was the one on Mântuleasa Street. What memories do you have of that?

·E· The discovery of books, of reading; that most of all. At about ten I began reading novels, detective stories, in fact all the sorts of things that one does read when one is ten or a little over. Alexandre Dumas in Romanian, for example.

·R· You yourself hadn't begun to write?

·E· I didn't really begin writing until my first year in high school.

·R· I know that you were passionately interested in science at that age.

·E· In the natural sciences, but not in mathematics. I compared myself to Goethe, because Goethe couldn't stand mathematics. And because, like him, I was in love with the natural sciences. I began with zoology, but it was entomology that especially interested me. I wrote some articles on insects and got them published in a magazine, the *Journal of Popular Science (Ziarul Stiintelor Populare).*

·R· An author by the age of twelve!

·E· Yes, I had my first article published when I was

11

thirteen. It was a sort of scientific story that I entered in a competition. It was sponsored by the *Journal of Popular Science* and was open to all high-school students in Romania. My little effort was called "How I Discovered the Philosopher's Stone." It won first prize.

·R· You mention that story in your *Journal*, I believe, and you say: "I've lost it, I shall never find it again, and how I would love to be able to reread it." Did you ever find it?

·E· I did! Yes! A man in Bucharest read my *Journal*, went to the Academy library, tracked it down, copied it, and very kindly sent it to me. I had remembered the theme and the way it ended but not the exact plot or the treatment. I was amazed to find that it was quite well told. Not at all pedantic, not "scientific." It was a real story. It was about a fourteen-year-old schoolboy—myself in fact—who has a laboratory and is making experiments because he is obsessed, like everyone, by the desire to find a way of transmuting matter. He has a dream, and in his dream he experiences a revelation: a being shows him how to fabricate the stone. He wakes up, and there in his crucible he finds a nugget of gold. He believes his transmutation has really worked. But later he realizes that it is only pyrites, fool's gold.

·R· It was the dream that led him to the philosopher's stone?

·E· It was in the dream that a being—a man who was at the same time like an animal, a transmuted being—gave me the formula. And I did as he told me.

·R· For a child to write such a tale, he would have to be interested in more than just insects; he'd have to be interested in chemistry and alchemy too.

·E· I was passionately interested in zoology, my specialty being insects; but I was interested in the physical sciences generally, and especially chemistry—inorganic chemistry in particular, before I became interested in organic chemistry. Odd, really.

·R· A dream, alchemy, the chimerical figure initiating

12

you: in your very first piece of writing we find figures and themes typical of your whole life's work. Does this mean that we possess a confused awareness, even in childhood, of who we are and where we are going?

·E·   I don't know. For me, the importance of that story is that as early as twelve or thirteen years old I could envisage myself working seriously, scientifically, with matter, the material world, yet felt drawn at the same time to imaginative literature.

·R·   Is that what you mean when you speak of the diurnal side of the mind?

·E·   Of the diurnal operation of the mind and the nocturnal operation of the mind.

·R·   Science on the daylight side, poetry on the dark side.

·E·   Yes, the literary imagination, which is both the mythical imagination and the revealer of the broad structures of metaphysics. Nocturnal, diurnal: both. It is the *coincidentia oppositorum.* The great whole. Yin and Yang.

·R·   In your case, there is the man of science on the one side, the writer on the other. But the two meet on the ground of myth.

·E·   Exactly. An interest in mythology and the structure of myths is also a desire to decipher the message of that nighttime life, of that nocturnal creativity.

The Attic

·R·   In short, even before you were out of high school, you'd already become—a writer!

·E·   In a certain sense, yes, since I had published not only a hundred or so short articles in the *Journal of Popular Science* but also a number of stories: impressions of my trips to the Carpathians, an account of a journey down the Danube and on the Black Sea, and, finally, some fragments

13

of a novel, *Novel of a Nearsighted Adolescent.* A wholly autobiographical novel. Like my central character, when I was undergoing a fit of melancholy—my Moldavian heritage—I fought back against my depression by using all sorts of "spiritual techniques." I'd read Payot's book *The Education of the Will* and tried to put his ideas into practice. Even at high school I had already begun what I later called my "war against sleep." That was because I wanted to make more time. It wasn't just science I was interested in, you see; there were lots of other things: I had discovered Oriental studies, then alchemy, then the history of religions. By chance I had read Frazer and Max Müller, and then, after I'd learned Italian—in order to read Papini—I also discovered the Italian Orientalists and historians of religion: Pettazzoni, Buonaiuti, Tucci, and others besides. And I wrote articles about their books or about the problems they were interested in. Of course I was very lucky as far as all that side went: I had an attic all to myself in the family home in Bucharest, quite separate from the rest of the house. So, when I was only fifteen years old, I could entertain friends, spend the whole evening—the whole night—up there, drinking coffee, discussing things. Since the attic was away from the rest of the family, the noise didn't disturb anyone. When I took full possession of my attic, I was sixteen. At first I had shared it with my brother; but then he left for the military academy, so I was left sole master of that space: two small rooms that suited me to perfection. I could read with impunity all night long. You know, at seventeen, when one is discovering modern poetry and so many other things, it's wonderful to have a room of your own, one that you can organize, transform, one that isn't just a place on temporary loan from your parents. So it really was *my* place. I lived up there, I had my bed, the colors I'd chosen. I had prints that I'd cut out and pinned on the walls. Above all, I had my books. It was more than a study: it was the space I lived in.

·R·   It sounds as though the gods, or the fairies, were watching over your first steps.

·E·   I think they must have been, because, really, I had every possible good fortune all the time I was still living at home.

·R·   When you went to the university, what was the intellectual atmosphere, the cultural atmosphere, like in Romania at that time, between 1920 and 1925?

·E·   We were the first generation to receive our cultural education in what at that time was called "greater Romania"—the Romania that emerged from the 1914–18 war. The first generation without an already established program, without a ready-made ideal to turn into a reality. My father's generation and my grandfather's had been presented with an ideal already formed: the unification of all the Romanian provinces. That ideal was now realized. And I was lucky enough to be part of the first generation of Romanians to be *free,* to have no set *program.* We were free to explore not only the traditional sources of culture—in other words, the classics and French literature—but all the rest as well. I had discovered Italian literature, the history of religions, and the East. One of my friends had discovered American literature; another, Scandinavian culture. We discovered Milarepa, in the Jacques Bacot translation. Everything was possible, you see. We were getting ready for a real breakthrough at last.

·R·   A breakthrough to the universal. India, a presence in people's minds; Milarepa, who was later read by Brancusi . . .

·E·   Yes, and at the same time, during those years between 1922 and 1928, we were also in the process of discovering Proust in Romanian, as well as Valéry and, of course, surrealism.

·R·   But how was that desire for the universal reconciled with a desire for Romanian roots? Or didn't you have that?

·E·   We felt that purely Romanian creations would be difficult to achieve within the climate and forms of Western culture that our fathers had loved: Anatole France, for

15

example, or even Barrès. We felt that what we had to say required a different language from that of the great authors and thinkers our fathers and grandfathers had thrilled to. We were attracted by the Upanishads, by Milarepa, even by Tagore and Gandhi, by the ancient culture of the East. And we thought that by assimilating the message of those archaic, non-European cultures we might find ways of expressing our own spiritual heritage, a heritage part Thracian, part Slav, part Romanian, and, at the same time, protohistorical and Oriental. We were very much aware of our position between East and West. As you know, Romanian culture formed a sort of bridge between the West and Byzantium, while also linking the Slavic world with the Oriental world and the Mediterranean world. The truth is, though, that I didn't become fully aware of all those possibilities until later on.

·R·   You mentioned surrealism just now, but you have said nothing about Dada or about Tzara, your fellow countryman.

·E·   We knew about them; we'd read their work in the avant-garde periodicals, which we found very exciting. But I personally wasn't influenced by Dada or by surrealism. I was astounded by them, and I admired, well, let us say their courage. But I was still recovering from the shock of futurism, which we had just discovered. I was fascinated, as you know, by Papini, the early Papini, before his conversion—the great pamphleteer, the author of *Maschilità,* of *L'Uomo finito,* his autobiography. For us, that was the avant-garde. I had also discovered Lautréamont, through Léon Bloy, odd though that may seem. I had read a collection of articles—*Belluaires et Porchers* perhaps it was—and in it there was an extraordinary article on *Les Chants de Maldoror,* with long quotations. That's how I discovered Lautréamont before discovering Mallarmé or even Rimbaud. I didn't read Mallarmé and Rimbaud until later, at the university.

·R·   In your *Journal* you speak several times about an "existentialist" climate in Romania, an existentialism that actually preceded French existentialism.

·E·   True, but that didn't happen until rather later, between 1933 and 1936. All the same, as early as my university days I had already read two or three of Kierkegaard's lesser works—in an Italian translation. Later I discovered the German translation of his work, which is almost complete. And I remember I wrote an article on him for a newspaper, *Cuvântul.* The article was called "Pamphleteer, Fiancé, and Hermit," and I believe it was the first article on Kierkegaard ever published in Romania. That was in 1925 or 1926. Kierkegaard meant a great deal to me, but above all as an example. Not only because of his life, but also because of what he heralded, what he anticipated. Unfortunately he was maddeningly prolix, which is why I think that Jean Wahl's *Etudes kierkegaardiennes* is perhaps . . . well, Kierkegaard's best book, because it's packed with very well-chosen quotations; all the essentials are there.

·R·   At the university you shared a certain number of enthusiasms with other young people of your generation; but what things did you find attracted you particularly, as an individual?

·E·   In the first place, Orientalism. I had tried to teach myself Hebrew, then Persian. I had bought grammars, done exercises. So, Orientalism. But also the history of religions, mythology. At the same time, I went on publishing articles on the history of alchemy, and that is what singled me out from my generation. I was the only one passionately interested in both the East and the history of religions. In the ancient East and the East of today as well, in Gandhi as well as in Tagore and Ramakrishna—I hadn't yet heard of Aurobindo Ghose at that time. I had read Frazer's *The Golden Bough,* like everyone interested in the history of religions, and later Max Müller. In fact, it was in order to read Frazer's complete works that I began learning English.

·R·   Was all this simply the result of a desire for wider cultural horizons? Or was it, perhaps unconsciously, already a quest—beneath a surface diversity—for the essential man, for what one might call the "paradigmatic" man?

· E ·　　I felt the need to tap certain sources that had been neglected until my time, sources that were there, in the libraries, that could be unearthed, but that had no spiritual or even cultural topicality at the time. I told myself that man, and even European man, is not solely man as presented by Kant or Hegel or Nietzsche; that there were other, deeper veins to be mined in the European tradition and in the Romanian tradition. I felt strongly that Greece is not just the Greece of its admirable poets and philosophers but also that of Eleusis and Orphism, a Greece that had its roots in the Mediterranean and Near East of ancient times. Now, some of these roots, equally deep—since they penetrated right down into protohistory—I could also see in Romania's own folk traditions, which reach back to the immemorial heritage of the Dacians and, even before them, to the Neolithic peoples who once occupied our present territory. I was perhaps not actually conscious of seeking for exemplary man. But I did sense the great importance of certain forgotten wellsprings of European culture. That was the reason why, during my last year at the University, I began to study the hermetic and "occult" elements (the Kabbala and alchemy) in the philosophy of the Italian Renaissance. That was the subject of my thesis.

· R ·　　Before coming to your thesis, I should like to ask you about the personal reasons that led you to become a student of religions. The ones you've just indicated are of an intellectual order. But what about your inner relationship with religion?

· E ·　　I was somewhat ignorant of my own tradition, that of Eastern Christianity. My family was "religious"; but, as you know, religion in the Eastern Christian tradition is, above all, an acquired custom, as it were, so that it is very little taught: one doesn't go to catechism classes, for instance. It is the liturgy, the liturgical life, the services themselves, the communal singing, the sacraments, that count. I took part in those things, just as everyone did, but it was in no way essential to my life. My interest lay elsewhere. By now I was a philosophy student; and as I studied the philosophers, the great philosophers, I began to sense that there was something missing. I sensed that it isn't possible to understand human destiny, and man's specific mode of being in the world, without some acquaintance with the archaic stages of religious experience. And I also had the feeling that I would find it hard to discover those roots in my own religious tradition, in the present-day reality of a particular church, which, like any other, was conditioned by a long history and by institutions of whose meaning and successive forms I was ignorant. I felt that it would be difficult to discover the true meaning and message of Christianity inside my own tradition alone. That was why I wanted to dig deeper. The Old Testament first, then Mesopotamia, Egypt, the Mediterranean world, and India.

·R· But was there no metaphysical unease underlying that process, no mystical crisis, no period of doubt or sudden burning faith? So many adolescents go through such a period of religious or metaphysical torment, yet you seem to have escaped that.

·E· Yes, I never experienced any great religious crisis of that kind. It's odd. . . . I wasn't satisfied, but I had no doubts, because my faith wasn't all that intense. I simply felt that the essential something I really needed to find and understand had to be looked for elsewhere, not simply in my own tradition. In order to understand myself. In order to understand. . . .

·R· Might one say, then, that your path was that of gnosis and *jñāna* Yoga?

·E· Perhaps, yes. Gnosis, *jñāna* Yoga.

·R· They are synonyms, I believe?

·E· Yes, exact synonyms. At the same time, I needed a technique, a discipline, something I couldn't find in my own religious tradition—though in fact I hadn't really looked for it. I could very easily have become a monk, retired to Mount Athos, and discovered all the techniques of Yoga there, couldn't I? Such as *prāṇāyāma,* for instance.

19

·R· Or hesychasm.

·E· Yes. But I didn't know that at the time. I felt the need for gnosis but also for some kind of technique, for a practical method of meditation. I hadn't grasped the religious value of our Sunday services in those days. I didn't discover that until after my return from India.

·R· We have left your thesis hanging in mid-air. What was its subject, exactly?

·E· Italian philosophy from Marsilio Ficino to Giordano Bruno. But it was Ficino who interested me particularly, Ficino and Pico della Mirandola. I was fascinated, not only by the fact that Greek philosophy had been rediscovered by these Renaissance philosophers, but also by the fact that Ficino had produced Latin translations of the hermetic manuscripts—the *Corpus hermeticum*—acquired by Cosimo de' Medici. I was equally excited by the fact that Pico knew Ficino's translation of those texts and that he had learned Hebrew, not just in order to understand the Old Testament better but, above all, in order to understand the Kabbala. So it was clear to me that these men's work involved not merely a rediscovery of Neoplatonism but also an extension of classical Greek philosophy. The discovery of hermeticism implied a breakthrough toward the East, toward Egypt and Persia.

·R· So you were excited by everything in the Renaissance that implied a breakthrough into areas that weren't specifically Greek or classical?

·E· I had the impression that this widening of the field indicated a much broader attitude of mind, a much more interesting and creative spirit than anything I'd found in the classical Platonism rediscovered in Florence.

·R· There was a certain analogy between that Renaissance, the Renaissance of the kabbalist, one might perhaps call it, and what was happening in your time in Romania: a conscious attempt to go beyond the frontiers represented by purely Mediterranean man, to participate in a cultural creation nourished by non-European traditions.

20

·E·   By a tradition.... Let us say by a "nonclassical" tradition rather than a "non-European" one, meaning a tradition lying deeper than the classical heritage handed down by our Thracian ancestors and by the Greeks and Romans. Later on I understood that what was involved was the fund of Neolithic culture that is the matrix of all the urban cultures of the ancient Near East and the Mediterranean world.

·R·   "Later on": by that you mean as a result of what you learned in India. But I'm amazed that you've made no mention of Nicolas de Cusa between Pico and Bruno.

·E·   I had made several visits to Italy, one of which lasted three months. That was when I discovered his *De docta ignorantia* and his famous observation regarding the *coincidentia oppositorum,* which acted like a catalyst on my own thought. But I didn't study him for my thesis, I didn't go any deeper into his work. To make up for that, when I began teaching, in 1934, back in Bucharest, I devoted a seminar to the *Docta ignorantia.* And Nicolas de Cusa still excites me even today.

The Renaissance and India

·R·   On 10 February 1949 you received a letter from your "old master Pettazzoni." He greeted the recent publication of your *Traité d'histoire des religions** in terms of warm approval, and you wrote back: "I remember those mornings in 1925, when I had just discovered *I misteri* and was hurling myself into the history of religions with all the passion and self-confidence typical of an eighteen-year-old. I remember the summer of 1926, when, having embarked on my correspondence with Pettazzoni, I was given a copy of *Dio* as a gift and went through it underlining almost every line. I remember . . . ."

·E·   Yes, I remember. I made several trips to Italy while I was a student in Bucharest. The first time I stayed

---

*The title of the English translation of this, published in 1958, is *Patterns in Comparative Religion.*

five or six weeks. I met Papini in Florence. In Rome I met Buonaiuti, the famous historian of Christianity, editor of *Ricerche religiose.* Then, in Naples, Vittorio Macchioro, at that time curator of the National Museum there, as well as being Italy's preeminent classicist and specialist in Orphism. Pettazzoni I didn't meet on that trip. I got to know him much later. But we did exchange letters.

·R·   It's not all that usual for a very young man to go and search out teachers in that way and to be so well received by them. But I suppose that it was the passion for knowledge that drove you on and, consequently, the necessity to go to the very source. Which also explains the reception you were given. What did you expect from Macchioro, for instance?

·E·   It was his central thesis that had interested me in the first place. He believed that he had discovered the stages of an Orphic initiation in the paintings unearthed in the "Villa dei Misteri" at Pompeii. He also believed that the philosophy of Heraclitus could be explained in terms of Orphism. In addition, he believed that Saint Paul was not solely a representative of traditional Judaism but that he had also been initiated into the Orphic mysteries and that, as a consequence, Paul's Christology had introduced Orphism into Christianity. This hypothesis had met with a poor reception; but I was only twenty, and to me it seemed very exciting. So I went to see Macchioro.

     I worked on my thesis partly in Bucharest, partly in Rome—in Rome mostly, in fact; but the majority of my documents, my notes, I kept in Bucharest. And while I was working on the thesis on Renaissance philosophy for my degree, I went on broadening my mind by getting to know the Italian Orientalists and historians of religion. I discovered Orphism with Macchioro and Giacomo de Flore with Buonaiuti. And I read Dante, whom Papini (and others) linked with "I fedeli d'amore." Ultimately, studying the Renaissance philosophers and studying religions were the same thing.

·R·   I imagine it wasn't just the reader of Dante who

interested you in Papini but the man, too, the literary volcano.

·E·   I had published several articles on Papini; I had also written to him and received a long letter in return that began: "Dear unknown friend." He commiserated with me on being a student of philosophy, "the most futile science invented by man." I gave him forewarning of my visit, and he received me in a tiny study crammed with books. I expected to meet a "monster of ugliness," which was how he had described himself in *Un uomo finito*. But despite his pallor and his "cannibal's teeth," Papini seemed to me majestic and almost handsome. He smoked incessantly while questioning me about my favorite authors and introducing me to books by a number of modern Italian writers I had never heard of. Then I questioned him, in my turn, about his intransigent, intolerant, almost fanatical Roman Catholicism (he was an ardent admirer of Léon Bloy); about his *Dizionario dell'uomo selvatico,* abandoned after publication of the first volume; and about his literary plans, particularly the book he had already announced several times: *Rapporto sugli uomini.* That same evening I wrote an account of my interview that was published by a magazine in Bucharest. I saw him again exactly a quarter of a century later, in May 1953. He was almost blind and had just broken off work on his magnum opus, *Giudizio universale,* in order to write *Il diavolo.* Once again I published a long account of the interview, this time in *Les Nouvelles Littéraires,* which gave him great pleasure, because he felt that his popularity in France had waned. Shortly after that, however, his blindness and increasing paralysis reduced him to the state of a living corpse. He survived for more than a year, continuing with savage determination to dictate his famous *Schegge,* which were published twice a month in the *Corriere della sera*—an almost miraculous feat in the circumstances.

·R·   You met Papini in Florence. But it was in Rome that your destiny was to a large extent determined.

·E·   Yes, it was in Rome, one day when I was in the library of Giuseppe Tucci's school while he himself was away in India, that I came across the first volume of *The History of Indian Philosophy* by the famous Surendranath Dasgupta. In the preface, Dasgupta had included a grateful tribute to his patron, the Maharajah Manindra Chandra Nandy of Kassimbazar. He wrote: "This man helped me to study for five years at Cambridge University. He is a true patron of the arts and letters. He protects and encourages both scientific and philosophic research; and his generosity is renowned throughout Bengal." I immediately felt a sort of intuition. I wrote off two letters there and then: one to Professor Dasgupta at the University of Calcutta, the other to the Maharajah in Kassimbazar, saying: "I am at present writing my degree thesis; I shall present it in October, and I wish to study comparative philosophy. I am therefore most anxious to learn Sanskrit and study Indian philosophy, particularly Yoga." Dasgupta was in fact the great specialist in classical Yoga and had written two books on Patañjali. Well, two or three months later, when I was back in Romania, I received two letters. One was from Dasgupta. It said: "Yes, it's a very good idea. If you really want to study comparative philosophy, then it would be better to learn Sanskrit and Indian philosophy here, in India, than in any of the major centers of Indian studies in Europe. And since you won't be able to obtain much in the way of a scholarship for that, I am writing on your behalf to the Maharajah." And the Maharajah's answer was in fact: "Yes, jolly good idea. Come. I'll give you a scholarship, but not for two years. [I had asked for only two years for fear of overplaying my hand.] You can't learn Sanskrit and Indian philosophy properly in two years. I am giving you a scholarship for five."

So that was how it happened. As soon as I had defended my thesis, in November 1928, and had become a newly fledged bachelor of arts, specializing in philosophy, I was given a little money by my parents and the promise of a scholarship from Bucharest University. I then set out from Constanza on a Romanian ship bound for Port Said, where I boarded a Japanese ship for the voyage to Colombo and from there went on by train to Calcutta. I broke my journey for two weeks in Madras, which was were I met Dasgupta.

·R· A wonderful story, and one that would round off our chapter nicely. But we need to know the rest. When you were on the ship, about to set out, what did you feel?

·E· I felt that I was . . . setting out! At twenty-one I was possibly the first Romanian who had decided, not just to travel to India, but to live and work there. I felt that I was setting out on an adventure, that it would be tough; but that excited me. Especially since I knew that I was not yet formed, complete. I had learned a great deal from my teachers in Bucharest and Italy, historians of religion, Orientalists, but I needed a new framework. I could feel that. I still wasn't a real grownup.

I stopped off for ten days in Egypt. My first Egyptian experiences . . . But the important thing was the journey itself. I had very little money, so I waited for the cheapest boat available, a Japanese ship that had a third-class berth available. It was on that ship that I began speaking English for the first time. It took us two weeks, the trip from Port Said to Colombo. But out there on the Indian Ocean I had already begun to encounter Asia! And discovering Ceylon, as it was called then, that was extraordinary. Twenty-four hours before landfall you could smell the scents of the trees, the flowers, strange new fragrances. . . .
So that was how I arrived in Colombo.

Interlude

·R·   When I arrived, a short while ago, you mentioned the idea that had just come to you for a title for these conversations of ours.

·E·   Yes, the title came to me as a result of my reaction, not to our dialogue, but to the fact that it's being recorded, which entails the constant presence of this machine, which for me is an ordeal, an "initiation ordeal," since I am unaccustomed to such things. So my title is: *Ordeal by Labyrinth*. Partly because all this is an ordeal from my point of view—the necessity to recall things by now almost forgotten. Partly because we go forward, then have to go back and start again, rather as though we were trying to find our way through a maze. And I think that the labyrinth is in fact the image par excellence of initiation. But apart from that, I also consider that every human existence consists of a series of initiatory ordeals or trials; man creates himself by means of a series of unconscious or conscious initiations. Yes, I think that that title expresses very well what is happening from my point of view, confronting your recorder; but it also appeals to me because it is, in addition, a quite accurate expression, I feel, of the whole human condition.

·R·   I find your title excellent. As I came up the rue d'Orsel, I too was thinking about a title for these conversations. I had reread a few pages of your *Journal,* and I was thinking of Ulysses, of his experience in the labyrinth.

Ulysses in the Labyrinth? Perhaps that was overdoing the mythology? I rang your bell, and as you let me in you said . . .

·E· "I've thought of a title," yes.

·R· Was it just a coincidence? At all events, I prefer your title; it seems to me definitive. As for your ordeal by tape recorder, I am aware that it's a real struggle for you to overcome your distaste for the thing.

·E· Yes, I wonder why. Perhaps it's the idea that what I say, its very spontaneity, is immediately recorded, fixed. Or is it rather the fact that there is a censor, or rather an inanimate object, coming between us? A mere thing that is nevertheless playing an important role in the dialogue. It must be that—the fact that there is an object intruding into the dialogue and paralyzing me slightly.

·R· Isn't what bothers you rather the desire for perfection and an unpleasant feeling that you are uttering an incomplete, imperfect discourse, which the recorder is going to freeze into a kind of false perfection?

·E· No. My impression is that the very presence of the "machine" actually *causes* my expression to become imperfect. In other words, my expression is as good as I can make it. I know perfectly well that one can't express oneself with the same precision in conversation as in an article, a book. No, what makes me uneasy is the machine, that inhuman, physical presence.

·R· Well, we must just try to forget about it. And yet, the tape is recording things that the reader will be unaware of: the birds twittering among the leaves of the little square we can see from your window, the clacking of the pigeons' wings as they fly across it to perch beside a garlanded mask on a Greek pediment.

·E· Yes, the Théâtre de l'Atelier.

·R· How did you come to live in this apartment, on this square? Was it a conscious choice?

28

·E·   No, it was chance, a happy chance. I was looking for a pied-à-terre in Paris for vacations. But I liked it very much right away, this square, and the whole neighborhood.

·R·   Do you like the neighborhood just because of its atmosphere? Or is it the fact that Charles Dullin . . .

·E·   Yes, there's something in that, the mythology of the neighborhood. I was aware of that before I'd ever seen this house. But I think the square is very beautiful, and it really is a very lovely part of Paris around here. I don't mean just the famous bits up on Montmartre, but also certain streets, not far from here, that I'm very fond of.

·R·   We are between the Marché Saint-Pierre and Sacré-Coeur.

·E·   Sacré-Coeur and the Place des Abbesses, which is also very fine.

·R·   As a piece of architecture, Sacré-Coeur comes in for a lot of adverse comment these days.

·E·   Oh, I know, and I can't say I like its architecture myself, or the color of its walls. But it's wonderfully placed—the perspective, the space around it. It's a mountain, isn't it? And besides, you can't help being aware of Montmartre's history: it's there in front of you; and life around here hasn't changed all that much, fortunately. I was rereading the final volume of Julien Green's *Journal* recently, and I was struck by his constant insistence on the way the beauty of Paris is being destroyed. They cut down trees, they demolish magnificent eighteenth- and nineteenth-century houses, they build modern apartment blocks, which are more comfortable to live in, no doubt, but entirely without charm. It's true, a certain beauty that was peculiar to Paris is disappearing. But that's such a dismally hackneyed subject; let's not pursue it.

·R·   When shall we be able to read the book you refer to in your *Journal,* in the entry for 14 June 1967, about the structure of sacred spaces, the symbolism of dwellings, of towns and villages, of temples and palaces?

29

·E· It is only a small book, written as a result of the six lectures I gave at Princeton on the sacred roots of architecture and town planning. It goes back in a more specific way over the material relating to "the center of the world" and "sacred space" in my *Patterns in Comparative Religion* and other works. All that I have left to do on it is choose the illustrations. But I've been spurred on to finish the book by the anticipation some architects have expressed. I've had letters from them saying that my earlier books have given them valuable insights into the meaning of their profession.

·R· You say somewhere that the sacred is characterized by both orientation and meaning, which are both expressed by the French word *sens*.

·E· As far as geometry is concerned, up and down are identical; but from the existential point of view we know that to go down a staircase is by no means the same thing as to go up it. We know that left is not right. In this book I concentrate on the symbolism and rituals that relate to the way we experience the various *qualities* of space: left and right, the center, zenith and nadir.

·R· But isn't architecture equally bound up with time? With temporality?

·E· We find temporal symbolism expressed in the symbolism of architecture and in the individual dwelling. Among certain African tribes the hut is oriented differently according to the season of the year. And not just the hut itself but also the objects it contains: certain tools, certain weapons. The whole house changes with the seasons. That is an exemplary case of the interrelation between temporal symbolism and spatial symbolism. But archaic tradition is rich in similar examples. You must certainly recall what Marcel Granet calls "oriented space" in ancient China.

·R· Yes. And it isn't only the house that is "sacred," or the temple, but the territory, the land itself, the homeland.

·E· Every homeland constitutes a sacred geography.

30

For those who have left it, the city of their childhood and adolescence always becomes a mythical city. For me, Bucharest is the heart of an inexhaustible mythology. And through that mythology I have succeeded in getting to know its true history. And my own too, perhaps.

❧ The Essential India

The Apprentice Sanskrit Scholar

·R·   On 18 November 1948, you wrote in your *Journal:* "Twenty years ago today, at about 3:30 P.M. (I think!), I was at the railway station in Bucharest about to leave for India. I see myself again at the moment of departure: I see Ionel Jianu holding the book by Jacques Rivière and the box of cigarettes, his parting gifts. I had two small suitcases. The influence of that journey, made before the age of twenty-two: what would my life have been like without that experience of India as the threshold of my transition to early manhood? And the certainty I have had ever since: that, whatever happens, there is still a cave in the Himalayas waiting to welcome me." Are you able to answer it now, that question you asked in 1948? How important was India in your life and work? In what way did India affect your growth? If you don't mind, let that be the basic theme of our conversation today. So, when you reached Madras, was Dasgupta expecting you?

·E·   Yes, he was working on some Sanskrit texts in the library of the Theosophical Society, which is famous for its collection of manuscripts. That was where I met him, and we immediately made plans for my stay in Calcutta. In 1928 he must have been about forty-five. He was short, thickset, with slightly protuberant eyes—"frog's eyes," you might say—and a voice that I found very melodious, like those of Bengalis generally. And I became very attached to him; I admired him enormously.

·R·   Your relationship with Dasgupta—was it that of a student to a teacher or that of a disciple to his master, to a guru?

·E·   Both. In the beginning I was the student, and he was like a tutor at a British university. It was he who drew up my program of studies at Calcutta University, who gave me a list of all the indispensable grammars, textbooks, and dictionaries. It was he who found me my boardinghouse in the Anglo-Indian quarter. He thought, quite rightly, that it would be very difficult for me to start living like an Indian right away.

   I worked with him not only at the university but at his home, in the Bhowanipore district, the native quarter, which was very picturesque. He had a wonderful house there. Then, after a year, he suggested I work with a pandit (chosen by him) so that I could become accustomed to talking in Sanskrit. He told me that later on I would need to be able to talk in Sanskrit, even if only in an elementary way, in order to converse with the pandits, the real yogins, the Hindu monks.

·R·   What were the difficulties Dasgupta said you would encounter if you tried to live like an Indian right away?

·E·   He said that at first even eating an exclusively Indian diet was not really to be recommended. Perhaps he also thought that it would be difficult for me to live in the native quarter, in Bhowanipore, wearing the clothes I'd brought, which were plain enough but European. He knew that I couldn't go directly, in just a few weeks or even months, from European clothes to the Bengali *dhoti*.

·R·   But you yourself, you had this desire to live the daily life of the Bengalis, to adopt their diet, their costume?

·E·   Yes, but not at the very beginning, because I was wholly unfamiliar with that way of life. I went at least twice a week to Dasgupta's house to work with him. Then, little by little, the spell, the mystery of those vast houses with their

34

terraces, surrounded by palm trees and gardens, undoubtedly had its effect on me.

·R· Just now I saw the fine photograph of you that is to be reproduced on the cover of the *Cahiers de l'Herne.* Was that the garment you wore in Calcutta?

·E· No, it was in the *ashram,* in the Himalayas, that I dressed like that. What I am wearing in the picture you mention is the yellow-ochre robe of a swami or a yogi. In Calcutta I wore the *dhoti,* which is a sort of very long white shirt.

·R· Do you think that one experiences a country like India differently if one dresses as its inhabitants do?

·E· Yes, I do think it's very important. In the first place it's much more comfortable, in the tropical climate, to go about in a *dhoti* and either barefoot or in sandals. And also one ceases to be a focus of attention. Because I lived out in the sun, I was brown like everyone else, so I passed unnoticed, or almost. The children didn't run after me shouting: "White monkey!" It was also a way of expressing solidarity with the culture into which I wanted to initiate myself. My ideal was to speak perfect Bengali. I never managed that, but I could read it fluently. I translated some poems by Tagore, and I tried to read, and even to translate, the mystical medieval poets. It wasn't just the academic and philosophic side—Yoga and Sanskrit—that interested me, but living Indian culture too.

·R· So you didn't just experience India simply in an intellectual way. It was the whole man that was involved.

·E· Yes, the whole man. But I must make it clear that I hadn't abandoned my Western consciousness or, let us say, the *Weltanschauung* of the Westerner. I wanted to learn Sanskrit really properly, in the Indian way, but also using the philological method characteristic of the Western mind—to conduct my studies both according to the methods of the educated European and from within as well. I never renounced my specifically Western instrument of

35

knowledge. I had done a little Greek and a little Latin, I had studied Western philosophy. And I kept all that. Once dressed in my *dhoti,* or my *kutiar* in the Himalayas, I didn't reject my Western tradition. So, you see, my dream of combining contraries was there in the training stages too.

·R·   Just as it wasn't any metaphysical torment that turned you toward the study of religions, so it wasn't any predilection for the exotic, or a desire to lose your own identity, that led you to don the yellow robe of the ascetics. You retained your identity, your Western training, and you wanted to approach India through them. In order, ultimately, to fuse two points of view or, rather, to combine them into one organic whole.

·E·   That's it, precisely. And I studied Indian culture deeply, "existentially." At the beginning of my second year, Dasgupta said to me: "Now, yes, the moment has arrived for you to come into my house." I was there for a year.

·R·   Your intention wasn't solely to study Indian language and culture but also to practice Yoga. In other words, to know in your body, from personal experience, what the books on Yoga were really about.

·E·   Exactly. We shall come shortly to the practical experience of Yoga I set about acquiring in my *kutiar,* in the Himalayas. But already in Calcutta, in Dasgupta's house, I had said to him several times: "Professor! Please can't you give me just *something* more than the texts?" But he always replied: "Wait a little; it really is essential to know it all from the philological and philosophical viewpoint." Remember that he himself was a historian of philosophy, trained at Cambridge, a philosopher and a poet. But he was from a family of pandits, in a Bengali village, so that he was master of the entire traditional culture of such Indian villages. He would say to me: "Practicing Yoga is even more difficult for you Europeans than it is for us Hindus." Possibly he was apprehensive about the consequences. Calcutta is a huge city, and it really isn't very sensible to practice *prānāyāma,* breath control, in a city, where the air is always somewhat unhealthy. That's what I found out later, at Hardwar, on the slopes of the Himalayas, where the air is more suitable.

·R· How did you work with Dasgupta? How did you set about learning Sanskrit, first with him, then with the pandit?

·E· Well, as far as learning Sanskrit is concerned, I applied the method of the Italian Indianist Angelo de Gubernatis, which he describes in his autobiography, *Fibra.* It consists in working for twelve hours a day with a grammar, a dictionary, and a text. That's how he did it himself, in Berlin. Weber, his teacher, had said to him (this was in early summer): "Gubernatis, here is the situation: my Sanskrit course starts in the fall, but it's a second-year course, and we can't start at the beginning again just on your account. So you'll just have to catch up." Gubernatis shut himself away in a summer cabin, just outside Berlin, with his Sanskrit grammar and dictionary. Twice a week someone came to deliver bread, coffee, and milk. He was right, and I followed his example. Besides, I had already gone through two similar experiences, not quite so extreme, but still. . . . When I was learning English, for example, I used to work for several hours nonstop. But this time, right from the outset, I worked for twelve hours a day and on *nothing but* Sanskrit. The only exceptions I made were to take a walk now and then and to use my tea and meal breaks for improving my English: I could read it very well, but I still wasn't very good at speaking it. And while I was at Dasgupta's house, he would occasionally put questions to me or give me a passage to translate, just to monitor my progress. And, if it was rapid, I believe that was the result of my determination to study nothing other than Sanskrit. For a period of several months I didn't so much as pick up a newspaper or a detective novel—anything. And that exclusive concentration on a single object, Sanskrit, produced amazing results.

·R· All the same, isn't there a risk, using that method, of failing to acquire the subtlety and flexibility of the spoken language?

37

·E·   Certainly. But at the outset it was a matter of acquiring solid foundations, of absorbing the grammatical structures and concepts, the basic vocabulary. Later on, naturally, I applied myself to Indian history and aesthetics, to poetry and the arts. But to begin with, it is essential to aim at a methodical and exclusive acquisition of the rudiments.

·R·   I think I remember that Daumal saw Sanskrit as a method of philosophical training, as if the grammar of Sanskrit predisposes the student toward a certain metaphysics, leads him inevitably toward a knowledge of self and being. Do you feel that? What benefit did you derive from learning Sanskrit?

·E·   Daumal was undoubtedly right. Only, in my case, it was less the philosophical value or virtue of the language in itself that interested me—at least at first. What I wanted in the first place was to master it as a working tool so that I could read the texts, which weren't all of great philosophical value. It wasn't the Vedānta or the Upanishads that interested me at that time but, above all, the commentaries on the *Yoga Sūtras,* the Tantric texts—in other words, expressions of Indian culture less well known in the West precisely because their philosophy is not in fact on the high plane of that found in the Upanishads or the Vedānta. But they were what interested me, personally, above anything else, since I wanted to learn the techniques of meditation and mystical physiology, in other words Yoga and Tantra.

·R·   You learned Italian in order to read Papini, English in order to read Frazer, Sanskrit in order to read the Tantric texts. In every case, it seems, what you were after was direct access to something that interested you. The language was the path, never the goal. Doesn't that make you ask yourself a question? You could have become, not a historian of religions, of myths, of the imagination, but a Sanskrit specialist, a linguist. Another Eliade, an entirely different life's work, was possible. You might have become a Jakobson, a Benveniste, but bringing your own particular

38

bent to that field. One can't help trying to imagine what that other life's work might have been like! Were you ever tempted to set out along that path?

·E· Whenever I have attempted to learn a new language, it has been in order to acquire a new working tool. A language, for me, is the possibility of communicating: reading, speaking if possible, but, above all, reading. But there came a point, in India, in Calcutta, when I saw attempts being made to achieve a much broader comparative approach—comparing, for example, Indo-European cultures with pre-Indian, with Oceanic, with Central Asian cultures—and when I saw such extraordinary men of learning as Paul Pelliot, Przylusky, Sylvain Lévy, who knew not only Sanskrit and Pali, but Chinese, Tibetan, Japanese, and even the languages that were at that time termed Austro-Asiatic; and I was fascinated by that vast new world opening up to research: not just Āryan India but aboriginal India, and the opening-up of Southeast Asia and Oceania as a source of cultural material. I tried to make a beginning in that direction. Dasgupta dissuaded me. He was right. His intuition was right. But I did start to learn Tibetan from an elementary grammar, and I became aware that because it wasn't something I really wanted passionately, the way I'd wanted a knowlege of Sanskrit and English—or Russian and Portuguese later on—I didn't make very much headway. So then I got angry with myself, and I gave up. I told myself that I was never ever going to acquire the competence of a Pelliot or a Sylvain Lévy; that I was never going to be a linguist or even a real Sanskritist. The language as such, its structures, its development, its history, its mysteries, didn't have as much attraction for me as . . .

·R· As the images, the symbols?

·E· Exactly. Language, for me, was merely a tool, an instrument of communication, of expression. Later on I was very glad I stopped where I did. Because linguistics, after all, is an ocean. There is never any end to it: you have to learn Arabic and, after Arabic, Siamese; after Siamese, Indonesian; after Indonesian, Polynesian; and so on. I

39

preferred to read about the myths, the rituals associated with those cultures; to try to understand them.

Himalayan Yogin

·R·　In September 1930 you left Calcutta for the Himalayas. You left Dasgupta . . . .

·E·　Yes, after a quarrel, which I regret a great deal. He regretted it too. But at the time I felt there was nothing to keep me in a place where, without Dasgupta, I had no reason for being. I left for the Himalayas. I stopped off in several towns, but it was in Hardwar and Rishikesh that I finally decided to stay, because that is where the real hermitages begin. I was lucky enough to meet Swami Shivanananda. He spoke to the *mahant*, the superior, and he found a little hut for me, in the forest. The conditions were simple enough: I had to eat a vegetarian diet and not wear European clothes—they gave one a white robe. And every morning one "begged" for milk, honey, and cheese. I stayed there, at Rishikesh, for six or seven months—until April, more or less.

·R·　Rishikesh is in the Himalayas, but it isn't in Tibet?

·E·　You needed a visa to get into Tibet. But in 1929 I had spent three or four weeks in Darjeeling, in Sikkim, which borders on Tibet. The atmosphere there was already rather Tibetan. You can see the mountains of Tibet very clearly.

·R·　What sort of setting was your hut in?

·E·　Whereas Darjeeling is thousands of feet above sea level—an Alpine landscape in fact—Rishikesh is on the bank of the Ganges, though the Ganges at that point is still quite small; sometimes it is sixty yards across, then, quite suddenly, it's over two hundred, and in other places it's very narrow—twenty-five yards, ten yards. The banks were jungle, forest. In my day, there was nothing there but huts and a small Hindu temple. You never saw anyone. The huts straggled up the bank for a mile or two, about two hundred yards apart, sometimes a hundred and fifty, sometimes no more than fifty. From there you climbed up toward Lakshmanjula, the first stage of my pilgrimage, as it were. That was quite high up, and there was a series of caves occupied by monks, contemplatives, ascetics, yogins. I met several of them.

·R·   And how did you choose your guru?

·E·   It was Swami Shivananda, though at that time he was unknown; he hadn't yet published anything, but eventually he published something like three hundred books. Before becoming Swami Shivananda he had been a doctor, a physician, and a family man. He was familiar with European medicine, which he had practiced once, in Rangoon I think it was. And then, one fine day, he suddenly gave all that up. He shed his European clothes and made the journey from Madras to Rishikesh on foot. It took him almost a year. I found him interesting because he had been given a Western education. Like Dasgupta. He was a man who knew the culture of India through and through and could also communicate it to a Westerner. He wasn't particularly well educated in an academic sense, but he did have many years' experience of the Himalayas: he knew all the Yoga exercises, all the meditation techniques. And he was a physician, which meant that he understood our problems. So it was he who helped me a little with the practical side of breath control, meditation, contemplation. Of course I already knew all about them theoretically, because I had not only studied the relevant texts and commentaries but had also listened to other *saddhu* and contemplatives, in Calcutta, in Dasgupta's house, and in Santiniketan, where I had met Tagore; one had constant opportunities to meet people who had already practiced some particular method of meditation. So I already knew a little more than what is in the books, but I had never tried to put any of it into practice myself.

·R·   You used the word jungle just now. Does that mean we should imagine tigers and snakes?

41

·E·   I don't remember anyone ever mentioning that there were tigers roundabout, but there were a great many snakes, and there were monkeys, quite amazing monkeys. I seem to remember I glimpsed a snake on my third day in the hut. I was a little alarmed; I had the impression it was a cobra, so I threw a pebble at it, to frighten it away. A monk saw me do it and said to me (he spoke quite good English, he'd been a judge): "Why did you do that? Even if it was a cobra, there's nothing to be afraid of. No one can remember a single case of snakebite in this hermitage." I wasn't too sure I believed him, but I asked: "And down there, in the plain?" "Yes, down there, certainly, but not here!" Pure chance, perhaps? At all events, when I saw snakes after that, I just let them go by, and that was that. I never again tried to frighten away a snake with a pebble.

·R·   Almost fifty years have gone by since your days as a novice yogin, and now you are the author, a famous one, of three works on Yoga. One of them has, as its subtitle, *Immortality and Freedom*. Another is called *Techniques of Yoga*. What is Yoga? A mystic path, a philosophical doctrine, an art of living? Is its aim to confer salvation, or health?

·E·   To be honest with you, talking about Yoga hasn't interested me much for some time now. I have said everything on the subject that I felt it was important to say. I began with my dissertation, in 1936, called *Yoga: An Essay on the Origins of Indian Mystical Theology*. And I was criticized, quite rightly, for that word "mystical."

·R·   You had worked under Dasgupta's supervision, and he had even dictated his commentary on Patañjali to you, I believe?

·E·   Yes, but I'd been interested in the technical side of Indian spiritual education before that. I knew the speculative tradition, of course, from the Upanishads through to Śaṇkara—in other words, the philosophy, the gnosis, that had so excited the first Western Indianists.

Apart from that, I had also read books on the rituals. But I knew that there also existed, in addition to all that, a spiritual technique, a psychophysiological technique, that was neither pure philosophy nor a system of rituals. In fact, I had read works on Patañjali and also John Woodroffe's books (written under the pseudonym Arthur Avallon) on Tantrism. And I thought that with the Tantric method—which is to say, with that series of psychophysiological exercises that I just now called a "mystical physiology," because it tends to be based on an imaginary physiology—there was a chance of revealing a neglected dimension of Indian spirituality. Dasgupta had already presented the philosophic aspect of this method; but I thought it was important now to describe the techniques themselves and to present Yoga in a comparative perspective: side by side with the classical Yoga described by Patañjali in the *Yoga Sūtras,* the various "baroque," or marginal Yogas, as well as Yoga as practiced by the Buddha and Buddhism in India, then in Tibet, in Japan, and in China. That is why I wanted to acquire a personal experience of those practices, those techniques.

·R·   But is there no connection between that desire and the "war against sleep" you waged as an adolescent?

·E·   During my adolescence there was so much that I needed to read, and I felt that I was never going to get anywhere if I had to sleep for seven or seven and a half hours out of every twenty-four. So I began an exercise that I'm fairly sure I invented. Every morning I set my alarm clock for two minutes earlier. So in a week I gained a quarter of an hour. When I got down to six and a half hours of sleep a night, I stopped altering the time of the alarm for three months, so as to get really accustomed to that amount of sleep. Then I began again, still keeping to the two-minute reductions. I got down to four and a half hours a night. And then one day I had giddy spells, so I stopped. I called it, with true teen-age grandiloquence, "the war against sleep." Later on I read Dr. Payot's *The Education of the Will.* I remember that on one page he wrote: "Why shouldn't it be possible for us, by a simple operation of the will, to eat things that are made inedible for us merely by our cultural habits? Butterflies, for example, or bees, worms, maybugs. Or even a piece of soap." And I asked myself: "Yes, why not?" And I began "educating my will." But I'm afraid I probably misunderstood the book somewhat. At all events, I did try to overcome certain forms of distaste, certain tendencies that are natural to a European.

Yoga is in fact akin to such attempts. The body desires movement, so you immobilize it in a single position—an *āsana;* you cease to behave like a human body but like a stone or a plant instead. Breathing is naturally arhythmic, so *prāṇāyāma* forces you to breathe to a strict rhythm. Our psychomental life is in a constant state of agitation—Patañjali defines it as *cittavṛtti,* "whirlpools of consciousness"—so "concentration" enables one to control that whirling flux. Yoga is in a way a war against instinct, against life.

However, I wasn't drawn to Yoga for those reasons alone. No, if I became interested in such Yoga techniques, it was because it was impossible for me to understand India solely through what I had learned by reading the great Indianists and their books on Vedāntic philosophy, according to which the world is an illusion—*maya*—or through the monumental system of rituals. I couldn't understand—that way—the fact that India had produced great poets and wonderful art. I knew that somewhere there existed a third way, no less important, and that it entailed the practice of Yoga. Later on, in Calcutta, I heard it said, in fact, that such and such a professor of mathematics always took up an *āsana* when working and also made use of breath control—with beneficial results. And you know that Nehru, when he felt tired, used to take up the "tree position" for a few minutes. Such examples may sound on the face of it like mere gossip-column stuff, but it is indisputable that the science and art of controlling the body and mind are very important in the history of Indian culture and philosophy—in short, of Indian creativity.

·R· I shan't ask you any more about the theoretical aspects of Yoga; a few words here could be no substitute for the books you've written on the subject. I would rather ask you about your personal experience of it and what contribution it made to your life subsequently.

·E· If I have been somewhat unforthcoming about my apprenticeship in Rishikesh, it is for reasons that you can easily guess. But one can talk about certain things all the same—for example, about the first *prāṇāyāma* exercises I performed, under my guru's supervision. Sometimes, when I had succeeded in controlling the rhythm of my breathing, he stopped me. I didn't understand why. I felt perfectly well, I wasn't at all tired. He told me: "Yes, you *are* tired." You see, it was important to be guided by someone who was both a doctor and also familiar with the practice of Yoga from personal experience. And I became convinced that those techniques really do work. I even think I succeeded in understanding certain problems better. But, as I said just now, I don't want to go into that. Because, well, if we do face up to that question, it means saying everything, which in turn means going into details that would require long explanations.

·R· All the same, can I ask you if you were able to obtain any verification regarding the miracles or marvels that are said to result from the practice of Yoga? In one of your books you mention the youthfulness that yogins retain late into life. You suggest that meditating in a different, expanded time scale produces an extraordinary longevity in the body itself.

·E· One of my neighbors, a *naga,* or naked monk, was over fifty, and he had the body of a man of thirty. He did nothing but meditate all day, and he ate extremely little. I myself never reached the stage at which such things are possible. But any doctor will tell you that the healthy diet and way of life observed in such monasteries will prolong physical youth.

45

·R· And those stories about wet, icy sheets that are draped around the meditator and that dry several times during the night?

·E· Several Western observers have witnessed that. Alexandra David-Neel, for example. In Tibetan it is called *gtumo*. The body produces an extraordinary heat that can, as you say, dry the sheets. There is extremely reputable written evidence concerning this "mystical heat," or rather this heat produced by what is termed the "subtle physiology." The experience of the icy wet sheets drying very quickly on a yogin's body—yes, that is certainly a reality.

A Poetic Truth about India

·R· You expressed your Indian experience not only in your essays but also in your novels: *Midnight in Serampore* and *Bengal Night.* And also in *Isabelle and the Waters of the Devil,* which has not been translated from the Romanian and which you wrote, you told me earlier, as a means of releasing the pressure that built up inside you as a result of your intensive method of learning Sanskrit.

·E· Yes, after six or seven months of Sanskrit grammar and Indian philosophy I took a break; I was hungry for more imaginative fodder. I went to Darjeeling, and I began the novel you've just mentioned, which was autobiographical to some extent and somewhat fantastic. I wanted to find a way into the imaginary world that was obsessing me and get to know it. I wrote the book in just a few weeks. And I recovered my health and mental balance.

·R· It tells the story of a young Romanian who travels across Ceylon, visits Madras, stays in Calcutta, and meets the devil.

·E· He arrives in Calcutta and lives in an Anglo-Indian boardinghouse, like the one I stayed at. And also staying there are a number of young people who are fascinated by all sorts of problems. Then comes the intrusion of the "devil," and a whole series of things happens because the main character is obsessed by the "devil."

46

·R· In *Midnight in Serampore,* as in *The Secret of Doctor Honigberger,* there is likewise a fantastic element.

·E· Those two stories were written ten years later. In between *Isabelle* and the two novellas there was another more or less autobiographical novel, *Bengal Night.*

·R· I should like to linger for a moment over *Midnight in Serampore.* How far do you believe in the events you narrate? Those characters reliving the past, is that pure fantasy? Or do you believe in it a little? Because one does hear odd stories sometimes, doesn't one? And from very reliable people.

·E· I believe in the reality of experiences that cause us to "step out of time" and "out of space." During the past few years I have written a number of stories employing this possibility of stepping out of one's historical moment or of finding oneself in a different place, as in the case of Zerlendi. In describing Zerlendi's Yoga exercises in *The Secret of Doctor Honigberger,* I included certain pieces of information, drawn from my own experiences, that I omitted from my books on Yoga. At the same time, however, I added other, inaccurate touches, precisely in order to camouflage the true data. For example, there is mention of a Serampore forest, whereas in fact there is no forest there at all. So that if anyone tried to check the plot of the story *in concreto,* he would find that the author is not acting simply as a reporter, since the setting is an invented one. He would then be led to conclude that all the rest is invented—imaginary—too, which isn't the case.

·R· Do you think that what happens to the characters in *Midnight in Serampore* could happen in fact?

·E· Yes, in the sense that one can have an experience so "convincing" that one is forced to regard it as real.

·R· At the end of *The Secret of Doctor Honigberger*—a scholar who did in fact exist, and whom you quote in your *Patañjali and Yoga*—the reader may hesitate over which of

47

several possible keys to the enigma is the true one. What would your choice be?

·E· It may be quite obvious to some readers, since the character telling the story states that he is Mircea Eliade, a man who has spent several years in India, has written a book on Yoga . . .

·R· The narrator, you mean; but he doesn't actually say that his name is Eliade, does he?

·E· No, but Mme Zerlendi writes to him: "You who have spent several years in India . . . ." Well, in those days, what other Romanian had gone to India, had written on Yoga? The narrator must therefore be Eliade. And Zerlendi, being clairvoyant, was aware that, by some mischance, the extraordinary document he had concealed, in the hope that someone would one day decipher it and thereby be convinced of the reality of certain facts relating to Yoga— well, that document has just been deciphered by someone who not only knows Sanskrit and is familiar with Yoga but is also a novelist who will be tempted to tell this amazing story—as of course I did. And so, in order to remove all risk that someone might try to check the authenticity of the story—since it would be easy to identify the house and find the manuscripts in the library—in short, in order to prove that the whole thing is merely a literary fantasy, Zerlendi alters the whole appearance of his house, spirits away the library, and persuades his family to claim that they don't recognize the narrator. All this so that the document I was going to summarize in my story would not be regarded as authentic.

·R· I'm not sure that what we are saying will be terribly clear to those who haven't read the book. But so much the better, as long as their puzzlement leads them to find out for themselves what it's all about. As for me, I no longer know what to think. I feel I am in the situation of the characters listening to the "old man" in your last novel. You have an almost devilish gift for throwing your listeners off the scent, for twisting and turning your plots so that one becomes unable to tell true from false, left from right.

48

·E· That's true. I even think it is a specific characteristic of at least some of my prose writings.

·R· There is something impish about the pleasure you take in slightly bewildering your questioner, isn't there?

·E· Perhaps that is part of a certain educational method. One mustn't provide the reader with a perfectly transparent "story."

·R· An educational method, yes, but also because you have a taste for labyrinths?

·E· And it's an initiation test as well.

·R· Very well, let's leave your readers poised on the threshold of your labyrinths in Serampore forest and Zerlendi's Indian library. In *Bengal Night,* on the other hand, there is no fantastic element at all. And what moves me most, when I think back over the book—and it is a book one needs to think back over, since its content is revealed less while one is reading it than when one ponders, later, over what one has read—what affects me most vividly in the story is the image, the evocation of the young girl, the very presence of desire. The story is a very simple one, but it shines and burns with a beauty that creates desire, like the cave paintings of Ajanta, like Indian erotic poetry. Looking back now, how do you see it yourself?

·E· Well, it's a semiautobiographical novel. So, as you must realize . . .

·R· I realize that you like to draw the same veil of silence over both the mysteries of gnosis and the mysteries of love. But since we have mentioned the Ajanta paintings, can you tell me whether that connection, between the very sensual descriptions in *Maitreyi* (*Bengal Night*) and the Ajanta paintings, has ever been made before? And, if so, what was your reaction?

·E· Yes, it has been made. In a charming letter he sent me after reading the book, Gaston Bachelard wrote about its "mythology of sensual pleasure." I think he was right, because its sensuality is, in a sense, transfigured.

49

·R· That observation ties in exactly with an entry in your *Journal* made on 5 April 1947, in which you refer to the Ajanta paintings. You wrote: "The sensuality of those fabulous images, the unexpected importance they give to the feminine element! How could a Buddhist monk 'free' himself from the temptations of the flesh when surrounded by so many superbly naked figures, so triumphant in their beatific plenitude? Only a Tantric version of Buddhism could encompass such a eulogy of woman and sensuality. Someday it will be understood how important a role Tantrism played in revealing to the Indian consciousness, and impressing upon it, the value of 'forms' and 'volumes' (the triumph of the most languorous anthropomorphism over the original aniconism)." The erotic content of *Bengal Night,* your interest in Tantrism, and your insight into Indian art—one can see them all combined in that one entry.

·E· Yes. And seeing the Ajanta paintings was also the starting point of my growing love for Indian figurative art. I have to admit that Indian sculpture bewildered me at first. It was a work by Coomaraswamy that enabled me to grasp the meaning of that tremendous accumulation of detail. Not content with depicting a particular god, Indian sculptors throw in all kinds of signs, human figures, mythological figures. Not an empty square inch anywhere! It didn't appeal to me. And then I came to understand that the artist is absolutely intent on *peopling* that universe, that space he is creating around the central image. I realized that he is determined to *make it come alive.* And I came to love that sculpture.

To be more precise, if I felt a great love for Indian art, it was because it is an art of symbolic meanings, a traditional art. It was not the artist's intention to express anything "personal." He was sharing with everyone else the unitary universe of spiritual values specific to the Indian genius. It was a symbolic and traditional art but spontaneous too, if I may put it like that. Drawing on a common source never hampered the flowering of distinctive forms, never prevented variety. And that is true of all the arts.

In India, the music of Bengal was the only kind that I had any opportunity to become familiar with. But it was more particularly the plastic arts—paintings, monuments, temples—that interested me. They didn't interest me solely as "works of art." For example, the temple is an architectural creation with a very coherent symbolism, one whose religious function, with its attendant rituals and processions, is extremely closely integrated into the architecture as such. Moreover, in India, as in all eastern European villages some thirty or forty years ago, the "objet d'art" was not something one hung on a wall or shut away in a display cabinet, you know. It was a thing that you used: a table, a chair, a vase, an icon. It was in this sense that Indian art held such interest for me: the folk art as well as that of the temples, the sculptures, the paintings. Because of its integration into everyday life.

·R·   And Indian literature?

·E·   Well, I was very fond of Kalidasa. He was my favorite, perhaps. He is the only poet I really mastered, even though his Sanskrit is really quite difficult. His poetic genius is without peer. Among modern writers, I read some of the avant-garde authors, such as Acinthya, for example, a young Bengali novelist (young in 1930) very much influenced by Joyce. And, of course, Rabindranath Tagore.

·R·   It was Dasgupta who introduced you to Tagore, I believe?

·E·   Yes, I had the great good fortune to visit Tagore several times, in Santiniketan. I made copious notes after our conversations and also notes on everything that was said about him, the man and the poet, in Santiniketan. He was enormously admired, but there were those who criticized him, and I wrote all of it down. I hope that my "Tagore notebook" still exists, in Bucharest, even though my library has been moved several times. I admired Tagore for his attempt to combine all the possible human qualities and virtues in his own person. He was not only an excellent poet, an excellent composer (he wrote some three thousand songs, of which hundreds, I'm quite sure, are "popular songs" in Bengal to this day), a great musician, a good novelist, a master of conversation.... Even his life had a certain specific quality of its own. It wasn't an "artist's life," like D'Annunzio's or Swinburne's or Oscar Wilde's. It was a rich, complete life, open to the whole of India, to the whole world. And Tagore was interested in things that one would never have supposed could hold any interest for a great poet. He participated in community affairs, he was passionately involved in the school he'd started in Santiniketan. He had never become cut off from the folk culture of Bengal. One is very aware of how important the peasant tradition is in his work, even though it is obvious that he also drew inspiration from Maeterlinck, for example. And he was very good-looking. He was enormously successful; it was whispered that he was a Don Juan. Yet, at the same time, he radiated a spirituality that expressed itself in his body, his gestures, his voice. The body and face of a patriarch.

·R· You have painted a fine portrait of him, one that evokes a Bengali da Vinci or Tolstoi. And yet, in *Bengal Night,* you describe Tagore rather more . . .

·E· . . . critically, yes. I was expressing the attitude of the younger generation in Bengal. I had friends at the university, young poets, young teachers—well, because they were reacting against their fathers' generation, they regarded Tagore's work as showy stuff, no better than D'Annunzio's; as misty . . . not profound. Today, in India, he is perhaps neglected slightly because of the great stature of Aurobindo, or of Radhakrishnan, who is a great scholar. But I'm sure he'll be rediscovered.

·R· It is difficult to mention Tagore and leave out Gandhi.

·E· I did see Gandhi and heard him, but from a distance and not all that clearly: the loudspeaker wasn't working, or maybe there just wasn't one that day. It was in Calcutta, in a park at a nonviolent demonstration. But I admired him—as everyone did. I was concentrating on other problems, but the success of his campaign of nonviolence was something I cared about deeply. Needless to say, I was 100 percent anti-British. The British repression of the *swaraj* militants infuriated me, disgusted me.

·R· In short, you shared the feelings of your character in *Bengal Night:* loathing of the colonizer and even of the European?

·E· Yes, sometimes I was truly ashamed to be recognized as a white; I was ashamed of my race. I wasn't English, luckily, and I came from a country that had never had any colonies, from a country that had in fact been treated like a colony itself for centuries. So I had no reason to have an inferiority complex. But, simply as a European, I did feel shame.

·R· Were you very much concerned with "politics"—to put it at its simplest—in your young days?

·E· In Romania, not at all. I became politically aware in India. Because there I witnessed the repression. And I said to myself: "How right the Indians are!" It was their country; all they were asking for was a kind of autonomy, and their demonstrations were completely peaceful. They weren't attacking anyone, just demanding their rights. And the police repression was pointlessly violent. So it was in Calcutta that I became aware of political injustice and at the same time realized the spiritual possibilities of Gandhi's political activity: the spiritual discipline that made it possible to stand up to blows without hitting back. It was like Christ; it was Tolstoi's dream.

·R· So you were won over, heart and soul, to the cause of nonviolence . . .

·E· And of violence too! For example, one day I heard an extremist talking, and I had to admit he was right. I understood perfectly well that there had to be some violent protesters too. But it's true, I was deeply impressed by the campaign of nonviolence. And besides, it wasn't just an extraordinarily clever piece of tactics; it was an admirable

53

form of mass education, a way of teaching people how to achieve self-control in every sense. It was really more than just politics—I mean more than politics as we mean it today.

India's Three Lessons

·E· I was still under twenty-two when I arrived in India. That's very young, don't you think? And the next three years were essential ones in my life. India was my education. Today, if I try to formulate what the decisive lesson was that I learned there, I see that it was threefold.

First, the discovery that there existed an Indian philosophy, or rather a spiritual dimension, that was neither that of classical India—let us say, that of the Upanishads and Vedānta, of the monist philosophy, in short—nor that of religious devotion or *bhakti*. Both Yoga and Sāṃkhya profess dualism: matter on the one hand, spirit on the other. However, it was not this dualism as such that interested me; it was the fact that, in both Sāṃkhya and Yoga, man, the world, and life are not illusory. Life is real, the world is real. And one can master the world, gain control of life. What is more, in Tantrism, for example, by performing certain rituals, which must be prepared for by the use of Yoga over a long period, human life can be transfigured. It is a question of transmuting our physiological activity—for example, sexual activity. In ritual union, love is no longer an erotic act or merely a sexual act, it is a kind of sacrament; just as drinking wine, in a Tantric experience, is not simply drinking an alcoholic beverage but taking part in a sacrament. So, I discovered this other dimension, which wasn't well known among Orientalists generally. I discovered that India had a knowledge of certain psychophysiological techniques that enable man to enjoy life and at the same time gain control of it. Life can be transfigured by a sacramental experience. That was the first point.

·R· "Transfigured life." Is that the same as what you refer to elsewhere as "sanctified existence"?

·E· Ultimately, yes, it's the same thing. It is a matter of perceiving that by means of this technique—and by other

54

paths or methods as well—one can resanctify life, resanctify nature.

The second discovery, the second part of the lesson I learned, is the meaning of symbols. In Romania I hadn't been particularly attracted to religion; to my eyes, all those icons in the churches seemed merely to clutter them up. I didn't exactly regard the icons as idols, of course, but still . . . . Well, in India I happened to live for a time in a Bengali village, and I saw the women and girls touching and decorating a *lingam*, a phallic symbol, or, more precisely, an anatomically very accurate stone phallus; and, naturally, the married women at least could not be unaware of what it was, of its physiological function. So I came to understand the possibility of "seeing" the symbol in the *lingam*. The *lingam* was the mystery of life, of creativity, of the fertility that is manifested at every cosmic level. And that manifestation of life was Shiva, not the anatomical member that we know. So this possibility of being religiously moved by the image and the symbol—*that* opened up a whole world of spiritual values to me. I said to myself: it is clear that in looking at an icon the believer does not perceive simply the figure of a woman holding a child; he is seeing the Virgin Mary and therefore the Mother of God and Sophia, Divine Wisdom. This discovery of the importance of religious symbolism in traditional cultures—well, you can imagine its importance in my training as a historian of religions.

As for the third discovery, you could call that "the discovery of Neolithic man." I was fortunate enough, shortly before I left the country, to spend a few weeks in central India—the occasion being a sort of crocodile hunt—among the Santali aborigines; in other words, among pre-Āryans. And I was deeply struck by the realization that India still has roots going down very deep, not just into its Āryan or Dravidian cultures, but also into the very subsoil of Asian culture, into aboriginal culture. It was a Neolithic civilization, based on agriculture; in other words, on the religion and the culture that accompanied the discovery of agriculture, particularly the vision of the world of nature as an unbroken cycle of life, death, and rebirth: a cycle specific to vegetable life but one that also governs human life and at the same time constitutes a model for the spiritual life. So then I recognized the importance of Romanian and Balkan folk culture. Like that of India, it was a folk culture, based on the mystery of agriculture. Of course, in eastern Europe the expressions of it had been Christianized: for example, wheat was thought to have originated from drops of Christ's blood. But all such symbols have a very archaic, Neolithic, foundation. Indeed, thirty years ago, from China right across to Portugal, there still existed an underlying unity, the spiritual unity inherent in agriculture, guaranteed by agriculture, and thus by the Neolithic heritage. This cultural unity was, to me, a revelation. I discovered that even here, in Europe, our roots go far deeper than we had hitherto supposed, deeper than the Greek or Roman or even Mediterranean worlds, deeper than the world of the ancient Near East. And those roots reveal to us the fundamental oneness not merely of Europe but of the entire ecumene that stretches from Portugal to China and from Scandinavia to Sri Lanka.

·R· One becomes very aware—for instance, when one reads the first chapter of your *History of Religious Ideas*—how important to your thinking, to your work, that *revelation* was—that discovery, that confrontation with Neolithic man, with the "primitive" man behind Indian man. However, would you care to clarify the effect it had on you?

·E· In India I discovered what I later came to refer to as "cosmic religious feeling." That is to say, the manifestation of the sacred in objects or in cosmic rhythms: in a spring of water, in a tree, in the springtime of the year. This religion, still a living thing in India, is precisely what the biblical prophets were fighting against. And quite rightly, since Israel was the vessel of another religious revelation. Mosaic monotheism entails personal knowledge of a God who intervenes in history and who, unlike the gods of the polytheistic religions, makes his power manifest in ways not solely confined to the rhythms of nature, to the action of the cosmos. As you know, this type of cosmic religion, which we call "polytheism" or "paganism," was being treated with

56

scant respect when I was a young man, not only by theologians but also by some historians of religion. But now I had lived among pagans—among people who were able to participate in the sacred through the mediation of their gods. And those gods were figurations or expressions of the mystery of the universe, of that inexhaustible source of creation, of life, and of sacred joy. That gave me a starting point, so that I was then able to grasp their importance for the general history of religions. In short, it was a question of revealing the importance and the spiritual value of what is called "paganism."

As you know, the Prelithic and Paleolithic eras lasted possibly as long as two million years. Very probably, the religion of those archaic men was analogous to the religion of the primitive hunter. Relationships became established—relationships at once existential and religious—first, between the hunter and the quarry that he must needs pursue and kill; second, between the hunter and the "Lords of the Beasts," divinities who protected both quarry and huntsman alike. For this reason, it is very likely that the primitive hunter accorded great religious importance to bones, to the skeleton, to blood. And then, perhaps twelve or fifteen thousand years ago, came the invention of agriculture. It increased and guaranteed man's food resources and, as a consequence, opened the way for all the developments that followed: increase of population, construction of villages, then towns—in other words, urban civilization and all the political innovations of the ancient Near East.

The discovery of agriculture—and this was not its least important consequence—made possible a particular kind of religious experience. For example, there was the link between the fertility of the earth and the fertility of woman. The Great Goddess is the Earth Mother. So woman acquired enormous religious importance—and economic importance as well—because of her mystic connection with the earth, the guarantor of fertility and thus of life. And as I indicated a moment ago, it was also thanks to agriculture that man grasped the idea of the cycle—birth, life, death, rebirth—and endowed his own existence with value by integrating it into the cosmic cycle. It was the Neolithic man who compared the human condition, for the first time, to the life of a flower, the life of a plant. The primitive hunter had felt himself magically linked to the animal he hunted; now, with the discovery of agriculture, man acquired a mystical solidarity with plant life. The human condition shared the destiny of the plant, in other words an infinite cycle of births, deaths, and rebirths. Of course, things are more complex than that, since we are talking about a religious system that incorporates all the symbolisms of fertility, death, and rebirth—the Earth Mother, the moon, plant life, Woman, and so on—a system that, I believe, contained the seeds of all the essential forms to be found in all the religions that succeeded it.

What we also find is that with agriculture came the blood sacrifice. For primitive man, the animal *is there* in the world, it is *given*. Whereas the food plant, the edible seed, is not given. It had not just *been there* since the beginning of the world. Man *creates* a harvest, by his own toil and his own magic. In comparison with the hunter, that is a huge difference, because archaic man believed that nothing could be created without a blood sacrifice. We are dealing here with an extremely ancient and almost universal concept: the belief that all creation implies a magical transference of life. By performing a blood sacrifice, one is projecting the energy—the "life"—of the victim into the work one wishes to create. And it's quite odd, when you think about it: the hunter, when he slaughtered his quarry, never talked of murder. Certain Siberian tribes ask the bear's forgiveness and tell him: "It was not I who killed you, it was my neighbor, the Tungus, or the Russian." In other regions they would say: "It wasn't me, it was the Lord of the Beasts, who gave us permission." The hunters didn't recognize themselves as responsible for the killing. Among Paleolithic agricultural tribes, on the other hand, the myths about the origin of food plants all introduce a supernatural being who has agreed to be slaughtered so that the plants in question may grow from his body. They couldn't imagine any creation

without a blood sacrifice. And indeed, all the evidence in-
dicates that blood sacrifices, and human ones particularly,
were performed solely by agricultural communities. Never
by hunters. In short—and this was what was important for
me to understand—an entire spiritual universe was revealed
as a result of the discovery of agriculture. In the same way,
yet another universe of spiritual values became possible
with the advent of metal-working. I wanted to understand
the religious world of archaic man. For example, during the
Paleolithic period the hunter hadn't the slightest glimmer-
ing of the man-plant relationship, any more than he had of
the religious importance of woman. But once agriculture
had been invented, then woman's place in the religious
hierarchy became very considerable indeed.

·R·   Another striking thing is that in both cases—the
concept of the man-plant relationship and the introduction
of sacred killing—the central feature is the relation to death,
a particular relation to death. And it is also quite clear that
these two great symbolic axes can also be found in the
Christian world: seed that must die to be reborn, killing of
the Lamb, bread and wine held to be the body of the sacred
victim. Your account of "Neolithic man" provides much
food for thought. All the same, as you have said, this discovery does not throw light on "religious man" alone: it enabled you, by a roundabout route, to find your way back to
things nearer, more familiar to you, such as the peasant tradition of Romania. Would you have written that piece on Brancusi that I'm so fond of, for example, without your Indian
experience? Brancusi was a Romanian, a modern artist and the
father of a certain kind of modernity, yet at the same time
he was a Carpathian shepherd. Would you have understood
Brancusi in the same way if you had never had that contact
with the primordial origin of civilization in India?

·E·   Perhaps not, as you say. You have summed up
very well what I think on that point. As I grasped the profound oneness that underlies and unites aboriginal Indian
culture and Balkan culture—and the peasant culture of
western Europe, too—I felt that I had come home. As I

59

studied certain techniques, certain myths, I found myself back in Europe while still in Asia. I never felt that I was dealing with "exotic" things. As I observed the folk traditions of India, I began to perceive that the same structures are also present in the folk traditions of Europe. I think that did help me a great deal in coming to understand that Brancusi hadn't *copied* the creations of Romanian folk art. On the contrary, what he did was to find his way back to those self-same wellsprings from which Romanian and Greek peasants had drawn their inspiration in the first place, and so he rediscovered the extraordinary vision of a man for whom stone *exists,* a rock *exists* in a . . . let us say "hierophanic" way. He rediscovered archaic man's world of values from the inside. Yes, India, did help me, to a great extent, to grasp the importance, the autochthonous quality and, at the same time, the universality, of Brancusi's creative process. If you really dig down, down to the roots that reach right back into the Neolithic world, then you are very Romanian, or very French, while at the same time universal. It's a problem that's always fascinated me: how to rediscover the fundamental oneness, if not of humankind, then at least of a certain common civilization in Europe's past. Brancusi did succeed in rediscovering it. So, there you have it: that discovery, and that problem, bring the subject of India's influence on my life full circle.

Eternal India

·R·   The interest, the ever growing interest it would seem, that Westerners are taking in India, in Yoga, does it often look to you like a counterfeit coinage of the Absolute?

·E·   Even though there are abuses, exaggerations, excessive publicity, it is still a very important experience. The psychological concept of Yoga foreshadowed Freud and our discovery of the unconscious. Indian wise men and ascetics were in fact almost forced to explore the dark areas of the mind. They had observed that the effects of the physiological, social, cultural, and religious conditioning could be easily discerned and, as a consequence, brought under control. But the really important obstacles to the ascetic and contemplative life arose from the activity of the unconscious, from *samskāras* and *vāsanās,* that is, from "impressions," "residues," "latencies," which constitute what depth psychology denotes by such terms as "unconscious contents," or "structures," or "impulses." It is easy enough to combat worldly temptations, it is easy enough to give up family life, sexuality, bodily comforts, social life. But just when you think you are at last master of yourself, suddenly the *vāsanās* well up, and you are once more the "conditioned man" you were before. That is why a knowledge of the systems of human "conditioning" could never be an end in itself, either for Yoga or for Indian spirituality in general. The important thing was not just to know about the "conditioning" systems but to gain control over them. So they worked away at the contents of the unconscious in order to "burn them off." For Yoga, unlike psychoanalysis, considers it possible to control the impulses of the unconscious.

That is only one aspect, however. There are others. It is to anyone's advantage, in fact, to learn the technique of Yoga; because it isn't a mystique, or a form of magic, or a means of maintaining health, or a theory of education; it is a complete, original system, and one that works. The important thing is not being able to stop one's heart for a moment, for example—which, as you know, is possible; it is not being able to suspend one's breathing for so many minutes. No, its great advantage lies in enabling one to experience, through personal experiment, the utmost limits of the human body.

It therefore seems quite clear to me that this interest in Yoga is very important and that it will have happy repercussions and consequences. Of course, all those depressing works of "popularization" one sees . . . .

·R· I know that there you mean no criticism of men like Allan Watts, whom in fact you knew personally . . .

·E· Yes, quite well in fact. He had a genius for divination as far as certain Oriental traditions were concerned.

61

And he knew his own religion through and through, at first hand. As you know, he had been a Church of England priest. He was extremely well versed in both Western Christianity and Zen, and he had a considerable grasp of many other things. I admired him a great deal. Apart from which, he also possessed a rather rare gift: he knew how to express himself in unpretentious language, one that was not that of superficial popularization and yet very accessible at the same time. I don't think that Watts ever really abandoned his priesthood; rather, he went on seeking for another way of communicating to modern man what men of earlier ages termed "God." He became a master, a true guru, for the hippie generation. I wasn't an intimate friend of his, but I believe that he was an honest man, and I admired his power of divination. On the basis of just a few elements, using just a few good books, he was capable of presenting you with the essence of a doctrine.

·R· And what did he, Watts, think of your books?

·E· He read them, he quoted from them. He never criticized me for not being more "personal" in my work. He perceived quite clearly, in fact, that my aim was simply to render intelligible to the modern world, Western and Oriental—to people in India and Tokyo as well as Paris— certain religious and philosophical creations that were previously either little known or else misconstrued. For me, an understanding of traditional religious values is the first step toward a spiritual awakening. Whereas Watts, and others like him, believed—and maybe they're right—that one can speak directly to the masses with something resembling a "message" and awaken them that way. I myself believe that we are "condemned"—products of the modern world that we are—to receive any revelation solely through culture. It is through cultural forms and structures that we have to rediscover our sources. We are "condemned" to learn and to reawaken to the life of the spirit through books. In modern Europe there is no longer any tradition of oral teaching or folk creativity. That is why I believe that the book has an enormous importance, not only cultural, but also religious, spiritual.

·R· So you are not one of those teachers who burn books—or affect to do so?

·E· Indeed not!

·R· And yet, somewhere in there, along with the university teacher and the writer, perhaps the hermit of Rishikesh, the contemplative, is still awake, and waiting. Let me recall the quotation I made at the very beginning of this long talk we've had about India: "The certainty I have had ever since: that, whatever happens, there is still a cave in the Himalayas waiting to welcome me." Do you still think about it today, that cave?

·E· Oh yes! Still! That is my great hope.

·R· And what would you do there? Dream, read, write, or what?

·E· If the cave still exists—and it does exist, if not at Rishikesh, then at Lakshmanjula or Bhadrinath—and if I can still find it . . . . A cave in the Himalayas is freedom and solitude. I think that is enough: one is free, but one isn't cut off; one is cut off only from the world one has just abandoned, if one does abandon it. Above all, it is the feeling of freedom I had and that I think I would have again.

·R· This conversation about India is drawing to a close, and you have rounded it off by referring to *freedom.* That puts me in mind of an entry in your *Journal,* the one for 26 January 1961, which particularly struck me when I first read it: "I think that my interest in Hindu philosophy and ascesis can be explained as follows: India has been obsessed by *freedom,* by absolute autonomy. Not in any naïve, superficial way, but with full regard to the numberless forms of conditioning to which man is subjected, studying them objectively, experimentally (Yoga), and striving to find the tool that will make it possible to abolish or transcend them. Even more than Christianity, Hindu spirituality has the

63

merit of introducing Freedom into the Cosmos. A *jīvan-mukta*'s mode of being is not *given* in the Cosmos; on the contrary, in a universe dominated by laws, absolute freedom is unthinkable. India has the merit of having added a new dimension to the universe: that of free existence."

·E·   Yes, I would still say that today.

Interlude

·E· Yes, I have had dreams that I now think were very important to me. "Initiation" dreams, in the sense that later on, when I came to understand their meaning, I learned a great deal and acquired a certain confidence. I came to feel that I am not guided but aided: the self being aided by an unconscious self.

·R· Have you ever regularly written your dreams down, over a period of time?

·E· Yes, during a summer in Ascona. As you know, the famous Eranos gatherings in Ascona were organized by Olga Froebe-Kapteyn, who was a passionate devotee of Jungian psychology. It was she who suggested the experiment to me. I made notes every morning for a month. That enabled me to perceive that my dreams really did have a certain continuity. I think I kept the notebook, in which I also noted down the date of every dream. On occasion I told some of them to the psychologists who were there, and I sometimes made a note of their interpretations.

·R· Do you think that someone who wants to know himself, and to improve himself, ought to write down his dreams, sometimes?

·E· I can't judge. But I do think it's always useful to write down a dream. I remember once, when I was rereading one of my diaries, I came across a dream I'd written down ten years before. Well, it became clear to me as I reread it that the dream in question had in fact foreshadowed something very precise, something that did later happen. So I do think it's a good idea to record dreams, not simply in order to verify certain things, but also in order to increase one's self-knowledge.

·R· In your case, it is not a matter of "premonitions" but of a deeper level of knowledge?

·E· I believe that in such dreams, which I can sometimes recall very clearly, one is being given an autorevelation of one's own destiny. It is one's destiny that is revealed, in the sense of an existence being directed toward a precise goal, an enterprise, a work that one ought to accomplish. It is a matter of your deep destiny and therefore of the obstacles you are going to encounter, too; of serious, irreversible decisions you are going to have to make.

·R· In two of the dreams you have included in the published excerpts from your *Journal,* it is memory that is the central theme. In one you have put away certain precious objects but have forgotten where. You feel threatened by this loss of memory, you kneel in front of your wife, who is the only person who can save you. And I will quote your own account of the other dream: "Two old men, each dying, each alone. Their deaths will mean the disappearance, forever, leaving no trace, no witnesses, of an admirable life-story (which I, however, knew). Terrible sadness. Despair. I withdrew into an adjoining room and prayed. I said to myself: if God doesn't exist, then everything is finished, everything is absurd."

·E· I noted down other dreams too, or at least episodes from them. For example, the one in which I saw stars falling and turning into brioches. I went around handing them out to people, saying: "Eat them while they're hot!" But it is obvious that if I included those two dreams in particular when I was making my selection, it was because they seemed important to me. Loss of memory is something that does in fact obsess me. I used to have an extraordinary

66

memory, and I feel it's not as good any more. And I have always been obsessed by loss of memory in the sense of the disappearance of a past, of a history that I alone know.

The dream about the two old men . . . . If God doesn't exist, then everything is dust and ashes. If there is no absolute to give meaning and value to our existence, then that means existence has no meaning. I know there are philosophers who do think precisely that; but for me, that would be not just pure despair but also a kind of betrayal. Because it isn't true, and I know that it isn't true. If one reaches the stage of thinking it is true, that is a crisis so deep that it goes beyond personal despair: it is the world itself that is "smashed," as Gabriel Marcel put it.

Possibly one can see in those dreams my fear, my terror, of a heritage just disappearing. What is happening to those two old men may happen to Europe, with its millenniums-old spiritual heritage—because Europe's roots reach right back into the ancient civilizations of the Near East. That heritage may vanish. And that would be a loss, not just for what we call Europe, but for the whole world. That is why I was so struck with terror by the despair of those two old men, dying all alone without being able to hand anything on. It is very possible that our heritage, instead of being received and enriched by other cultures, may be despised, ignored, and even destroyed. It goes without saying that atomic bombs can destroy libraries, museums, and even whole cities in a very real way. But a particular ideology, or ideologies, can annihilate them equally well. Perhaps that is the truly great crime against the spirit; because I still believe that culture, even what is termed profane culture, is a creation of the spirit.

·R·   So when you talk of the European heritage being lost, despised, you are forcing us to picture our own culture becoming like one of those that Europe itself has pillaged, shattered, and whose memory you labored to preserve. And there are a number of very disturbing pages in your *Journal* on this very theme: you envisage our countries occupied by peoples who no longer have any idea of what our cultures, our books, were like.

67

·E·   Yes, that would be a spiritual and cultural tragedy. We have indeed pillaged other cultures. Fortunately, however, there have been other Westerners who have deciphered the languages, preserved the myths, salvaged certain artistic masterpieces. There have always been a few Orientalists, a few philosophers, a few poets striving to safeguard the meaning of certain exotic, extra-European spiritual traditions. But I can still picture a terrible possibility: an absolute contempt, or indifference, where such values are concerned. I can picture a society in which no one will have the slightest interest in a Europe that has been destroyed, forgotten, dismissed. It is a nightmare, but it is a possibility.

✍ Europe

Return to Bucharest

·R·   Between your return to Romania and your arrival
in Paris there was a space of almost fifteen years. It is that
period, crammed with events, that we are going to talk
about today. First of all, however, why did you leave India
after only three years?

·E·   I had written a number of somewhat exalted letters home from Calcutta about my latest Indian discoveries,
and I had been living for six months in the solitude of an
ashram. My father sensed that I was intending to stay in India
for another three or four years, and he was afraid I might
never return, that I might choose the solitude of the monas-
tic life or marry an Indian girl. And I think his intuition
was correct. So, since it was up to him to renew my exemp-
tion from military service, well, that year, January 1931, he
simply did nothing about it. In the autumn he wrote saying
that I must come back home. My father had been an army
officer. He added: "It would be a disgrace for me personally,
and a great humiliation for the whole family, if my son became
a deserter." So I went home. I fully intended to return to
India later on, to continue my research. Meanwhile, I presented my dissertation on Yoga, and the university committee in charge of these things asked me to work on a
version for publication in French.

·R·   You were originally posted to an antiaircraft artillery unit, but because of your nearsightedness you ended

up doing staff work as an English interpreter. Your dissertation was published in Paris in 1936, under the title *Le Yoga: Essai sur les origines de la mystique indienne.* And before long you became a very famous author as well as a brilliant young university teacher.

Coping with Fame

·R·   Where shall we begin? With your fame?

·E·   Yes, "with my fame," because it taught me a great deal. I entered *Maitreyi* (*Bengal Night*) in a competition for unpublished novels. I won first prize. It was a love story and, at the same time, exotic. The book had a huge success, which surprised the publisher, and me, as well. It was reprinted a great many times. And, at twenty-six, I had become a "celebrity"; I was written about in the newspapers, recognized in the street, and so on. It was a very important experience, because it meant that I found out, very young, what it means "to be famous," to have "admirers." It's pleasant, but there's nothing very amazing about it. So for the rest of my life I was no longer tempted by it. And it is a temptation natural to all artists, all writers, I think. Every author hopes to have a great success some day, to be recognized and admired by the general reading public. I had it very early, that success; I was delighted by it, and it enabled me to write other novels that were not destined for anything like the same success.

    In 1934 I published *Return from Paradise,* the first volume of a trilogy that also comprised *The Hooligans* and *Vita Nova.* I wanted to paint a portrait of my own generation. The first volume did have a certain success. It was my view that the young, my contemporaries, were *hooligans* in the full sense of that word, people laying the foundations for a spiritual and cultural revolution—not a "political" revolution, perhaps, but certainly a real and concrete one. The characters were consequently all young: young writers, teachers, actors. And they were people who talked a lot. In short, a group portrait of a number of intellectuals and pseudo-intellectuals, slightly reminiscent, I think, of Huxley's *Point Counterpoint.* It was a fairly difficult book. The critics liked it, but it didn't repeat the success of *Maitreyi.* That same year I also published an almost Joycean novel, called *The Light That Failed.*

·R·   The same title as one of Kipling's books. Was that intentional?

·E·   Yes, because of a certain similarity between the two central characters. I've tried to reread the book several times since—impossible, I can't understand a word of it! I had been very impressed by an excerpt from *Finnegans Wake,* published under the title "Anna Livia Plurabelle," and I employed the stream-of-consciousness technique of *Ulysses*—for the first time in Romania, I believe. It was wholly unsuccessful. Even the critics didn't know what to make of it. It was totally unreadable.

·R·   This influence Joyce had on you, and the taste for the word as such that it presupposes, does surprise me, rather. It seems to me that up until then you had been more inclined to treat language as simply a means to an end. Were you writing poetry at this time?

·E·   In a sense, yes. But I ought to say that what I was interested in, first and foremost, when I decided to use the stream-of-consciousness method, was conveying the mental processes of a man who loses his sight for several months. It was within that "internal soliloquy," containing all he thinks, sees, and imagines in that darkness—it was there that I really tried to play with language, allowing myself total freedom. And that is why the book is almost incomprehensible. Yet the story is a very simple one, and quite affecting, too. A librarian is working at night in a municipal library, correcting proofs—of a Greek text on astronomy, I think it was; anyway, it was a somewhat mysterious text. He begins to be aware of the smell of smoke, becomes uneasy, sees a number of rats scuttling away, then smoke seeping into the room. He opens the window, opens the door, and in the reading room he sees a young woman lying naked on a big table. Standing over her is a professor of Slavic languages,

71

reputed to be a creature of the devil, a magician. At the height of the fire, the professor vanishes. The librarian picks up the young woman, who has fainted, and rescues her. But as he is carrying her down the marble staircase, a section of molding on the ceiling comes loose, falls, strikes him on the head, and deprives him of his sight for six months. In the hospital he begins struggling to understand. It all seems absurd. Midnight, in the library of a university city, a fully clothed professor and a naked woman, a woman he knew quite well, as a matter of fact—she was the professor's assistant. The librarian now hears it rumored that the professor was performing a Tantric ritual and that the ritual was the cause of the fire. Then he recovers his sight, and in his joy at being able to see again—to see, not to read—he decides to go traveling. I don't recall the end exactly, because, as I said, I've never managed to reread the whole book. I know that at one point the librarian begins talking Latin to people who haven't had his education and so can't understand him—an echo of Stephen Daedalus perhaps? Everything becomes mysterious, enigmatic. At all events, the book was unreadable and a total failure. After that third book I was free. People still knew my name, but as the author of *Bengal Night*. I was freed from the necessity to please people.

·R·   One has only to read the entry for 21 April 1963 in your *Journal* to realize the extent to which that story was a personal one. I shan't ask you about that entry, for obvious reasons. It is up to the reader's curiosity whether he wishes to look it up and see what I mean. Personally, I am glad to have watched those fascinating images swim up to the surface. Perhaps they may yet produce a fantastic story—one of those you are at work on at the moment, maybe? But let us return to your period of celebrity: are you also unconcerned with posterity, with being remembered? Is it a matter of indifference to you whether your work survives or not?

·E·   From time to time I tell myself that I may continue to be read, in Romania, by my fellow countrymen, not on account of my merits as a writer but because I have, after all, taught at Chicago, been published in Paris, and not many Romanians have been so fortunate. Of course, there is the great Ionesco, and Cioran. They will survive.

·R· All the same, you are a famous man. What is your reaction, for example, to the desire that many of your readers may have to meet with you? How do you live with the celebrity, or notoriety, that you enjoy?

·E· Fortunately, I am able to ignore them, since I live for eight months of the year in Chicago and a few months in Paris. Generally speaking, I don't accept invitations to congresses, to conferences, or even to most kinds of parties. So I remain oblivious to the very heavy burden that celebrity, or notoriety, can bring. I admire those who are strong enough to cope with the consequences of such fame—television appearances, interviews, reporters. I would find that very hard. It's not so much the time lost—talking to a journalist for an hour or attending the opening of a new exhibition of paintings, that's not so very terrible—it's being caught up, dragged in, trapped, by the publicity machine. Apart from which, I should be forced to keep saying things over and over again, on radio, on television, that I have no desire whatever to repeat yet one more time. I haven't that vocation, though I do admire those who are capable of fighting the good fight on that front as well.

University Life, *Zalmoxis,* and Criterion

·R· So, now you are a celebrated young novelist and, at the same time, an Orientalist. And I know that at first your university lectures were packed with people who'd read *Bengal Night;* then the taxing nature of the work discouraged the merely curious. You were appointed as assistant to Naë Ionesco.

·E· He was a professor of logic, metaphysics, and the history of metaphysics. He also edited a newspaper. He was a man who wielded great influence in Romania. Well, he handed over his course on the history of metaphysics to me, plus a seminar on the history of logic, and suggested that I

73

preface my history-of-metaphysics lectures with a course on the history of religions. So I talked about the problem of evil and salvation in Eastern religions, about the Indian concept of being, about Orphism and Hinduism and Buddhism. And I began my logic seminar with a very high-sounding theme: "On the Dissolution of the Concept of Causality in Medieval Buddhist Logic"! Not an easy seminar, but I did have a small group who attended it. After that I chose Nicolas de Cusa's *Docta ignorantia* and Book XI of Aristotle's *Metaphysics*.

·R·   You were teaching, and you also started the periodical *Zalmoxis*.

·E·   Yes, I thought, and still do, that there is no contradiction between scholarly research and cultural activity. I began doing the groundwork for *Zalmoxis* during 1936; but the first issue, which ran to almost three hundred pages, didn't appear until 1938. I wanted to foster scientific study of the history of religions in Romania. In academic circles, it still didn't exist as an autonomous discipline. For example, as I've just said, I was teaching the history of religions under the aegis of the history-of-metaphysics chair. And one of my colleagues was lecturing on myths and legends from a chair of ethnology and folklore. So, to convince university circles generally that it was really quite an important discipline in its own right and that we could make significant contributions to the field—given that we already had a number of scholars in Romania interested in the history of Greek religions, for example—I decided that we needed something like *Zalmoxis*. So I wrote to all the specialists—quite a few—that I knew in other countries. An international magazine, in other words, brought out in French, English, and German, with contributions from several Romanian scholars. We got out three issues. It was possibly Romania's first contribution to the history of religions on . . . well, let us say the European level.

·R·   I take it, then, that the texts you published later as a book, under the title *Zalmoxis, the Vanishing God,* first appeared in that magazine?

·E·   No, only "The Mandragora Cult in Romania."
The rest came from elsewhere. For example, the piece on
aquatic symbolism comes from *Images and Symbols.*

·R·   In your *Journal* you talk about "Criterion." What
exactly was that?

·E·   Criterion was a group we organized, made up of
people who aren't known abroad, apart from Cioran;
although Ionesco came to the meetings too, I think. They
were symposiums, as it were, with five speakers taking part.
We dealt with subjects that were very important at that
time—1933, '34, '35—in Romania: not only Gandhi, Gide,
Chaplin, but also Lenin and Freud. Quite controversial
subjects, some of them, as you can imagine. And also modern art, contemporary music, even jazz. We invited representatives of all sorts of movements. For "Lenin," there
were the usual five speakers: the chairman was a well-known
professor from the university; one of the other speakers was
Lucretiu Patrascanu, who was general secretary of the
Communist Party at that time; another was Belu Silber, a
writer on Communist theory; but there was also a representative of the Iron Guard, Poliproniade, and a representative of, let us say, the political liberal center, a man who
was also well known as an economist, philosopher, and
theologian: Mircea Vulvanescu. The meetings were run as
debates on a motion, and I think that type of dialogue was
very important. When I wrote *Return from Paradise,* I knew
inside that it was actually a kind of paradise we were losing
then, because in those years, 1933 and 1934, it was still possible to talk quite openly. Later on we didn't actually have
censorship in the strict sense, but we had to pick subjects
that were more exclusively cultural. The Criterion group
had tremendous repercussions in Bucharest. It was at one of
our meetings, in 1933, that existentialism, Kierkegaard, and
Heidegger were discussed for the first time. We felt we
were engaged in a crusade against the old fossils. We wanted
to remind our audiences that Picasso and Freud existed.
People had heard of Freud, naturally, but he still wasn't
talked about enough, and the same with Picasso. We needed

to discuss Heidegger and Jaspers. And Schoenberg. We felt
that culture ought to be an integral part of the city's life. We
all shared a conviction that just talking within the university
wasn't enough, that it was imperative for us to get down and
fight in the real arena. We believed that the newspaper
had become an acceptable intellectual weapon, as it clearly
already was in Spain, thanks to Unamuno and Ortega. We
no longer suffered from the inferiority complex that had
afflicted our teachers' generation. They didn't dare publish
articles in daily newspapers, only in academic periodicals.
We wanted to address ourselves to the broadest possible
public and inject some vitality into Romanian culture, because it was in danger of sinking into a creeping provincialism if we didn't. I wasn't the only one thinking like
that, naturally, and I wasn't the group's leader. We had all
become aware of the necessity for such an effort and of the
fact that we alone were in a position to make it, because we
were young and because we weren't afraid of certain unpleasant consequences—for one's university career, for
example.

London, Lisbon

·R·   In 1940 you left Romania. You went to London as
a cultural attaché.

·E·   King Carol's last government foresaw that
Romania was going to be in difficulty. It decided to send a
number of young university teachers abroad, as cultural at-
tachés and advisers. I was posted to England. I was there
during the London blitz. I used my memories of that period
in *The Forbidden Forest*. My first image was of a city bulging
with huge balloons—the barrage balloons intended to protect it from the German bombers. And the blackout, the
total darkness at night. After the terrible raid on 9 September, some of our legation's offices were moved to Oxford.
That night I saw fires that came straight out of Hieronymus
Bosch: a city burning, the sky in flames. I had a tremendous
admiration for the courage and resistance of the British, for
that titanic effort to build up their armaments from almost

nothing. That was why, both in London and in Lisbon, I always believed in an Allied victory.

When Britain broke off diplomatic relations with Romania, after the German invasion in 1941, I was transferred to Lisbon. I stayed there for four years. I worked, I learned Portuguese, really quite well. I began writing my *Patterns in Comparative Religion* in Romanian and also part of *The Myth of the Eternal Return.* I wanted to write a book about Camoëns: not simply because he was a poet I loved, but because he had lived in India and the *Lusiads* contains descriptions of Sri Lanka, Africa, and the Atlantic Ocean.

I'm very fond of Lisbon. That great square beside the vast Tagus estuary, a superb space, one could never forget it. And the city's pastel coloring, the blue and white everywhere. And, at dusk, music in all the streets, because everyone sings. It was a city somehow slightly to one side of history, of contemporary history anyway, outside the inferno of the war. It was a neutral city, so one was able to observe the propaganda being put out by both sides; but it was my particular job to monitor the neutral press. Apart from that, I dealt with cultural exchanges: lecturers, musicians, mathematicians, writers, and theater companies. Our ambassador appreciated the value of such things, but he wasn't much concerned with them personally. I lived rather on the fringes of our legation—fortunately. "Diplomatic" life is rather tedious, stifling, frustrating: you feel trapped inside a sort of inbred "family," constantly meeting the same members of the diplomatic corps over and over again. I couldn't have stood it for very long.

The Power of the Spirit

·R· That period, when you were away from Romania but still in Europe—in London, then Lisbon, and finally Paris—it was a tragic time for Europe and Romania and for much of the rest of the world: first the high tide of the Fascist regimes, the dark days of the war, then the collapse of Nazism and, in Romania, the setting-up of a Communist regime. You were a witness to those events, sometimes a direct one. How did you react to them?

·E· To me it was self-evident that the Allies would win. At the same time, when Russia entered the war, I knew that the victory was going to be a Russian victory, too. I knew what that would mean for the peoples of eastern Europe. I had left Romania in the spring of 1940, so that any information I received about what was happening there was always at second hand. But I feared a Soviet occupation, even a temporary one. One always fears a giant neighbor. Giants can be admired only from a distance. But the choice had to be made: despair or hope. And I am always against despair of that kind, political and historical despair. So I chose hope. I told myself that it was simply one more ordeal that had to be gone through—we are only too familiar with the ordeals of history—we Romanians, Yugoslavs, Bulgarians, all of us—because our existence has always lain between empires. However, there's no point in trying to give you a résumé of European history, is there? We all know it. Our situation is like that of the Jews when they were caught between the great military empires of Assyria and Egypt, Persia and Rome. One is always crushed. So I personally chose the biblical prophets as a model. Politically there was no solution, not in the short term. Only later, perhaps. The important thing, for me and all the other Romanian émigrés, was to know how to safeguard our cultural heritage, how to go on creating through this historical crisis. The Romanian people would survive, of course. But what could we do, abroad, to help it survive? I have always believed that culture, too, can provide a means of survival. Culture is not a "superstructure," as the Marxists believe: it is man's specific condition. One cannot be a man without being a cultural being. I told myself: we must go on, we must safeguard the few Romanian values that are in danger of being snuffed out in our country—above all, freedom of research; for example, the scientific study of religion, of history, of culture. When I came to Paris in 1945, it was in order to continue my research, to put the finishing touches to a number of books dear to my heart, particularly the *Patterns* and *The Myth of the Eternal Return*.

78

You asked me how I reacted to that tragic period. I told myself that we were undergoing a great crisis but that the Romanian people had lived through such things before in its history—three or four crises per century. Those at home would do whatever destiny permitted them to do. But here, abroad, it was essential not to waste one's time in political nostalgia and regret, hoping for an imminent intervention by the United States and so on. Then came the postwar years, 1946, 1947, 1948, and during that time I experienced the certainty that no resistance can carry any weight unless one actually *does* something. And the cultural thing was the only thing that one could do. So I, Cioran, and many others all decided to work, each according to his vocation. Which doesn't mean that we had cut ourselves off from our country. On the contrary. It was simply that there was no other way in which we could be of use. Of course, one can always sign a manifesto, protest in the press. That is rarely what is really needed. Here, in Paris, we organized a literary and cultural circle, the Morning Star (Luceafarul), a name taken from the title of a famous poem by Eminescu, and also a Romanian Research Center. We tried to maintain the culture of a free Romania and, above all, to publish texts that had become unpublishable in Romania itself: literature of course, but also historical and philosophic works.

·R· On 25 August 1947, you wrote in your *Journal:* "People tell me: one must take on the responsibility of one's historical moment. Today we are governed by the social problem or, more precisely, by the social problem as posed by the Marxists. It is therefore *necessary* to respond through one's work, in one way or another, to the historical moment one is living through. Yes, but I shall try to respond as Buddha and Socrates did: by transcending their historical moments and by creating others, or laying the foundations for them." You wrote that in 1947.

·E· Yes. Because, after all, one cannot regard Buddha and Socrates as "escapists." Each of them took his historical moment as his launching pad and responded to it. Only they

79

did so on another level and in another language. And they were the men who unleashed spiritual revolutions, one in India, the other in Greece.

·R· It is clear from your *Journal* that you are rather impatient with demands made on intellectuals to fritter away their energies in political agitation.

·E· Yes, when I know in advance that such agitation cannot produce any result. If I were told: "You must demonstrate every day in the streets, publish articles for three months, sign every single manifesto, after which, I don't say that Romania will be set free, but at least Romanian writers will be free to publish their poems or their novels," then I would do it, I would do all that. But I know that such activities, for the moment, cannot produce any immediate consequences. So one must direct one's energies judiciously and attack in the areas where one can entertain some hope of at least some repercussion, some echo. That is what a number of Romanian exiles did this spring, in support of the movement started in Romania by Paul Goma. They organized a press campaign that did achieve positive results.

·R· I had supposed that you felt a certain indifference to things political. But I see now that it is more a matter of a refusal to be distracted by illusions, of insisting on seeing things as they really are. Not indifference at all.

·E· No, it is not a question of indifference. And besides, I believe that at certain historical moments some kinds of cultural activity—literature and art especially—themselves constitute political weapons. When I think of the effect of Pushkin's poems . . . . I won't mention Dostoevski! But even some of Tolstoi's stories come to mind. I believe that, at a certain moment, what we do in the realm of art, of science, of philosophy, will have a political effect: alter man's consciousness, breathe a kind of hope into him. So I don't think that, by continuing to work and create, one is escaping from one's historical moment.

·R· One cannot help thinking at this point of a man like Solzhenitsyn.

·E·   I admire him enormously. I admire the writer, yes. But above all I admire his courage as a witness, the fact that he truly accepted the role of witness, like a martyr. (Incidentally, the Latin word *martyr* was the origin of the Romanian *martor,* meaning witness.) Fortunately he also possessed certain assets, the weight of his name alone, not just because of the Nobel Prize, but because of the huge popular success of his novels; and then, his vast experience . . . .

·R·   The entry in your *Journal* for 16 February 1949 has this to say about the relationship of the intellectual to politics: "Meeting in my hotel room of fifteen or so Romanian intellectuals and students. I had invited them to discuss the following problem: Are we agreed or not that *today,* and above all *tomorrow,* the 'intellectual,' because of his access to concepts, is regarded, and will be regarded increasingly, as enemy number one and that he is entrusted by history (as so often in the past) with a *political mission?* In the war of religions in which we are at present engaged, the enemy is embarrassed solely by 'elites,' which for a well-organized police force have the advantage of being fairly easily suppressed. In consequence, 'making culture' is today the only efficacious form of politics open to exiles. The traditional positions are reversed: it is no longer the politicians who stand at the concrete center of history but the great minds, the 'intellectual elites.' (Long discussion that I must summarize one day.)"

·E·   Yes, I think that passage does sum up perfectly what I have been trying to say. I do in fact think that the *presence* of the intellectual, in the true sense of the word— great poets, great novelists, great philosophers—I think that their very presence is terribly disturbing for a police state or a dictatorship, whether of the left or the right. I know, because I have read everything there is to be read on the subject; for example, what Thomas Mann represented to the Gestapo, to the German police. I know what a writer like Solzhenitsyn represents and what a Romanian poet represents; their physical presence alone is disturbing to dictators, and that is why I say to you that one really must go on creating culture. A great mathematician once asserted that if one day the world's five greatest mathematicians took the same plane to a conference and the plane crashed, next day there would be no one left to understand Einstein's theory. It's a slight exaggeration, but those "five" or "six" are inordinately important.

Encounters

·R·   During those years you met a number of eminent men, notably, Ortega y Gasset and Eugenio d'Ors.

·E·   I met Ortega in Lisbon. The fact was that though he no longer considered himself an exile he was still not ready to return to Madrid. He came to dinner with us quite often, and we had long talks. I admired him a great deal. I admired his capacity to keep on with his work despite all his problems, both personal and political. He was writing his book on Leibniz at that time. He was a man of scathing irony. Hearing him talk made one slightly apprehensive. An aristocrat. He spoke excellent French, and he preferred to speak French, even with Germans. Even, and above all, with a certain German journalist, who also spoke French very well as a result of spending ten years in Paris as the correspondent of a large newspaper. I ought to add that this German wasn't a Nazi: he had taken part in the plot against Hitler, and his family had been executed. I think Ortega was saddened by the fact that he was less well known in France than in Germany, where almost all his books had been translated. The only French translation, I believe, was of the *Essais espagnols,* published by Stock, which included *The Revolt of the Masses.* That is a piece one can still reread now; it is completely topical, because today the masses are affected more than ever by ideologies. Besides which, everything he had to say about history is still very interesting, as is what he had to say about "marginal" cultures: Spanish culture, for example, which is integrated into European culture to an extent, but not as Ortega would have wished. His campaign to reawaken the Spanish consciousness to a cer-

82

tain kind of Spanishness and Europeanness at the same time—I find that important. And he was a man who was already confronting the problem posed by machines. He saw that we have to achieve a dialogue with the machine. Yes, I admired him a great deal. He was not only a professor of philosophy, an excellent essayist, and a magnificent writer, as you know, but he was also a great journalist. He too believed, as my professor, Naë Ionesco, did, that the newspaper is the real arena of thought today, not periodicals or books, as was once the case. It is through newspapers, he believed, that one establishes real contact with the public, that one can influence it, "cultivate" it. In Spain, Ortega is still read, republished, written about. I don't know why he is so little known and translated in France.

·R· And d'Ors?

·E· I quite often took trips to Madrid to buy books, and that was where I had one or two, perhaps three, long meetings with Eugenio d'Ors. He was more immediately approachable than Ortega, always smiling. I think his great ambition was to become well known in France. It was the journalist of genius I admired in him, the dilettante of genius. I admired his literary elegance and his erudition. From that point of view, Ortega and d'Ors were very similar. They were both descendants of Unamuno, even though both differed from him on many occasions. I admired d'Ors' diary, the *Nuevo Glossario*. It was a daily account of his intellectual discoveries: every day he wrote a page describing exactly what he had discovered or thought that day—or the day before, I should say; and he published it as he wrote it. He'd made a vow never to repeat himself. I admired that determination to remain constantly alive to everything, the decision to ask himself new questions every single day of his life and attempt to answer them. It's an interesting work but totally unknown. The five or six volumes of the *Nuevo Glossario* are out of print in Spain and have never been translated. Apart from that, he had some fascinating insights into the manueline style of architecture, and there is of course his famous book on the baroque. In the same field, he wrote a sort of philosophy of style, *Cupola and Monarchy*. It's a philosophy of forms and of culture, worked out in traditional terms. There is a French translation of it. If you ever find it in a bookstall somewhere, buy it. It's most fascinating.

·R· What you haven't said is that Eugenio d'Ors admired Mircea Eliade.

·E· True. He knew *Zalmoxis,* and he'd liked *The Myth of the Eternal Return* very much. It was an appreciation fostered by an exchange of letters and also by several long conversations.

·R· On 3 October 1949, you wrote: "Eugenio d'Ors sent me a further article on *The Myth of the Eternal Return.* It is headed: 'Se trata de un libro muy importante.' More than any other critic whose reviews I've seen, Eugenio d'Ors is full of enthusiasm about the way I have thrown light on the Platonic structure of archaic and traditional ('folk') ontologies." You do add, however: "But I am still waiting for someone to understand the other aspect of my interpretation, the one dealing with the ritual abolition of time and, as a consequence, the necessity for 'repetition.' The conversations I have had on this point have been disappointing so far." Later on, d'Ors was also to express admiration for your *Patterns in Comparative Religion.*

·E· Yes, that was the last work of mine he was able to read. He died the following year, I think.

·R· You mentioned Unamuno earlier, in connection with Ortega and d'Ors.

·E· I didn't know him personally. He died in 1936, I think it was, and my first visit to Spain wasn't until 1941. But I had always held him in the highest regard. His work is extremely important, and one day it will be discovered everywhere. There is a particular kind of "existentialism" in it that appeals to me a great deal. And I love the great poet that he became, though that side of him wasn't truly revealed until twenty years after his death, when his last poems were finally published. Yes, he was a wonderful man, and his work is essential, because it succeeded in laying bare the "visceral" roots of culture. Unamuno, like Gabriel Marcel, insisted on the importance of the body. Gabriel Marcel used to say that philosophers ignore the body, that they ignore man as a being made flesh. Well, Unamuno too insisted on the spiritual importance of flesh, of the body, of blood, of what he called the "visceral experience of the spirit." And that was very original, very new. And also, of course, he had enormous talent as a writer, as a poet, a prose writer, an essayist.

·R· So these *Conversations* of ours may serve, among other things, to spur our readers on to reread these authors—Ortega, d'Ors, and Unamuno—who, despite being so little read today, are nevertheless great writers?

·E· Yes. Unamuno especially.

·R· In London you met a fellow countryman of yours who was quite famous at the time, then sank into relative neglect, but is now being republished: Matila Ghyka.

·E· Yes, Matila Ghyka was a cultural adviser at the Romanian embassy. Before I met him, I had, of course, read *The Golden Number,* but I didn't know his fine novel *The Rain of Stars.* I admired him a great deal, and despite the difference in age we became friends. He was prodigiously well read, not just as a scientist but also in literature and history. As you know, he had been a naval officer, then a naval attaché, first in Saint Petersburg, then in London. After the Second World War he became professor of aesthetics at the University of California at Los Angeles. Besides his personal work, he read at least one book a day. Which was why he subscribed to five different book clubs! His opinions were sometimes rather odd. For example, he believed that the war, which had just broken out, was the final confrontation between two orders of chivalry, the Knights Templar and the Teutonic Knights. One day he showed me a photograph of a fairly large family, posed on the very imposing front steps of a large chalet. At one of the second-story windows you could just make out the slightly blurred face of an old lady. In fact, Matila Ghyka informed me in his deep, calm voice, that old lady had been dead for several months when the picture was taken. I met him again in Paris in 1950. He'd just finished a detective novel that he was going to publish under a pseudonym. His last years were rather hard ones: he would translate any book Payot offered him and accept any kind of work, despite being over eighty.

At left, below: Mircea Eliade and his father in 1942 in Bucharest.

At left, above: With C. G. Jung at Ascona in 1952, at the Eranos conference.

This page: With Christinel, his wife, and professor Joseph Kitagawa at Nara, in Japan, in September, 1958.

At left, above: Cioran, Ionesco, and Eliade in 1977. (Photo Louis Moynier)

At left, below: Claude Bonnefoy, Claude-Henri Rocquet, and Mircea Eliade in the *place* Charles-Dullin in 1978. (Photo J.-Louis Moore)

This page: Mircea Eliade and his wife in Chicago in 1978.

Mircea Eliade talking with Claude-Henri Rocquet; in the study in his Paris apartment. (Photo J.-Louis Moore)

❧ Paris, 1945

Paris

·R·   In 1945 you elected not to return to Romania but to live in Paris. What were the reasons for those choices?

·E·   1945: Romania was on the theshold of a historical change that was almost a foregone conclusion—a brutal transformation, imposed from outside, of its political and social institutions. On the other hand, after the four years spent in Lisbon, I needed to be in a city where I had access to extremely well-endowed libraries. I had begun my *Patterns in Comparative Religion* in London, thanks to the British Museum, and continued work on it at Oxford, thanks to the magnificent university library there. In Lisbon I really hadn't been able to work at all. I moved to Paris for a while—for a few years, I imagined at the time—in order to resume work on that book and finish it. And immediately after my arrival I had the good fortune to be invited by Professor Georges Dumézil to teach a course of my own choice at the Ecole des Hautes Etudes. And it was George Dumézil again who introduced me to Gallimard, the publishing house, and who wrote the preface for my *Patterns.*

·R·   So you received a warm welcome from Professor Dumézil. However, as one can glean from certain entries in your *Journal,* the next few years were to be ones of great poverty and of great uncertainty about the future. It was also a time of intensely hard work, not only academic but literary as well. Can you tell us about that life as "a poor student," as you put it, and as a working scholar, as a man of learning and a writer?

·E· I wrote "poor" because I lived in a hotel room and made my own lunch on a gas ring. After our marriage, Christinel and I used to eat our meals in a small neighborhood restaurant. So I was in fact poor, in that sense. The big problem was my work and the fact that I now had to write in French. I was quite clear in my own mind, from the very start, that my French wasn't going to be the perfect French of Ionesco or Cioran but rather a French analogous to medieval Latin or to Koine, the Greek that was spoken and written during the Hellenistic period in Egypt and Italy—indeed, from Asia Minor to Ireland. The question of style held no terrors for me, as it did for Cioran. He worshiped the French language for its own sake; he regarded it as an artistic masterpiece in its own right and was determined not to humiliate such a marvelous language or inflict wounds on it. Fortunately for me, I didn't have those scruples. I just wanted to write French clearly and correctly—nothing more. I worked at that and produced several books in French, which of course a number of my friends went over for me, Jean Gouillard in particular.

·R· What were the books you wrote during that period?

·E· The *Patterns in Comparative Religion* was almost complete. I wrote *The Myth of the Eternal Return* and the first few articles that were later collected in *Images and Symbols.* Also a long article on shamanism for the *Revue d'histoire des religions,* a number of others for *Paru* and the *Nouvelle Revue française,* and one for the magazine *Critique,* at Georges Bataille's invitation.

·R· I know that Georges Dumézil was full of admiration for the way you were able to accomplish so tremendous a task of scholarship in such unfavorable conditions.

·E· Yes, he wondered how it was possible to produce a final draft of a work like the *Patterns*—or even a rough one!—in a hotel room. Well, that was how it had to be! Of course I went out to various libraries a lot, but a great deal of my time was also spent at my work table. Especially at night, because during the daytime there was the noise from the neighbors.

·R· Your scientific work was also bedeviled by another passion of yours: for reading—Balzac especially—and also for writing.

·E· Yes, I had always enjoyed Balzac, but then, being in Paris, I succumbed totally. I immersed myself in him. I even began writing a life of Balzac in Romanian, which I thought I might get published in Romania to mark the centenary of his death. I wasted a great of time on that venture, but I don't regret it. As you can see, Balzac is still there, on my shelves.

·R· And you began to write *The Forbidden Forest?*

·E· That was later, in 1949. But I had written a number of stories before that. Every so often I felt the need to rediscover my roots, my native land. In exile, the road home lies through language, through dreams. So I wrote stories.

·R· Hearing you talk today, there is no trace of the distress your deprivations at that time must have caused you. After all, you were not only living in very harsh circumstances, there was also the experience of being cut off from your past. And yet that loss, that severance, if we are to believe your *Journal,* seemed full of meaning for you at the time. Were you, perhaps, experiencing a sort of initiatory death and rebirth?

·E· Yes, as I told you earlier, I believe that the best expression and the most accurate definition of the human condition is as a series of initiation trials or ordeals—which is to say, of deaths and resurrections. And then, yes, as you say, I was suddenly cut off from my past; I was fully aware that for the time being I could neither publish nor write solely in Romanian. But, at the same time, I was experiencing

89

exile, and that exile, for me, wasn't entirely discontinuous with my past or with Romanian culture. I experienced my exile exactly as an Alexandrian Jew did his during the Diaspora. The Diaspora in Alexandria and Rome was in a sort of dialectical relationship with the homeland—Palestine. For me, my exile was still part of Romania's destiny.

·R·   I wasn't thinking solely of your exile but also of all you had lost: your manuscripts, for example, when you tried to reconstruct lost works from memory.

·E·   That loss—yes, I did feel that. I discovered later that a large part of my correspondence and manuscripts was missing. And then I accepted it. I reconciled myself to that loss. I began again. I went on.

·R·   In the Paris of 1945 you met, not the existentialists, but Bataille, Breton, Véra Daumal, Teilhard de Chardin, and, of course, the great French Orientalists and Indianists. There is no mention in your *Journal* of Sartre, Camus, Simone de Beauvoir, Merleau-Ponty . . . .

·E·   I read them, and I think I did make a lot of references to them; but when it came to choosing the excerpts—amounting to no more than a third, sometimes as little as a fifth, of the original manuscript of the *Journal*—I didn't keep the passages in which, for example, I wrote about Sartre's famous lecture "L'Existentialisme est un humanisme." I was there; but things of that sort are so well known already, so much a part of our cultural atmosphere, that I preferred to retain other passages. Apart from which, my relationships with Bataille, with Aimé Patri, possibly even with Breton, and with a number of Orientalists— Filliozat, Paul Mus, and Renou—were closer than with the existentialist philosophers. Bataille was determined to meet me because he had so much enjoyed the book on Yoga I had published in 1936. He turned out to be someone who was very interested in the history of religions. He was trying to map out a history of man's mental and spiritual development, and the history of religions was naturally a part of that

90

enormous undertaking. He was fascinated—and it was very important for me to know why—by the phenomenon of eroticism. We had long discussions about Tantrism. He asked me to contribute a book on Tantrism to his series for Editions de Minuit. I just never found the time to write it.

·R·   What is your opinion of Bataille's work?

·E·   I haven't read it all, so I hesitate to pass judgment. His thinking always stimulated me, and sometimes it irritated me. There were some things I rejected, and at the same time I was aware that my inability to accept them was due to my not quite having grasped everything he was saying. At all events, he was a very original mind, and important for contemporary French culture.

·R·   Did you perhaps meet Caillois and Leiris with Bataille?

·E·   Leiris no. But I did know Caillois quite well. I used his books and articles and quoted from them a great deal. What I found so attractive about him was his universalist, encyclopedic approach. He was a Renaissance man, just as interested in German Romanticism as in the myths of the Amazon, in the detective novel as in the art of poetry.

·R·   And Breton?

·E·   I admired him as a poet, as a man, and even as a physical presence. I used to meet him frequently at Docteur Hunwald's and at Aimé Patri's house. I used to stare at him, rather: I was so fascinated by that great lion's head of his. He was a man with an almost magical presence for me. I was amazed to find that he had read my little book on the techniques of Yoga. He, on his side, was amazed by the *coincidentia oppositorum* achieved by Yoga, which coincides, in turn, with the paradoxical situation he had described in his famous formula: "A point where up and down . . . cease to be perceived as contradictory." He was surprised and delighted to discover the Yoga version of the *coincidentia oppositorum*. He was interested in Yoga and Tantrism, as well

91

as in alchemy, which we often discussed together. He was intrigued by the imaginary world revealed in the alchemical texts.

·R· In your *Journal* you also mention meeting Teilhard de Chardin.

·E· I went to see him two or three times, in his room on the rue Monsieur, in the house of the Jesuit fathers. At that time he was totally unknown as a philosopher. His books couldn't be published, as you know. He published only scientific articles. We had long talks, and I was fascinated by his theory of evolution and the Point Omega, which, it seemed to me, actually went against Roman Catholic theology: taking Christ out to the furthermost galaxy—that seemed nearer to Mahayana Buddhism than to Christianity. But he was a man who interested me deeply, kept me spellbound. And I was delighted to read his books later on. I understood then how Christian his thought really was, as well as being both original and courageous. Teilhard was reacting against certain Manichean tendencies that have infiltrated Western Christianity. He clarifies the religious value of Matter and Life. And that made me think of the "cosmic Christianity" of the eastern European peasant, for whom the world is "holy" because it was sanctified by the incarnation, death, and resurrection of Jesus Christ.

Being Romanian

·R· Needless to say, you also saw a lot of the other Romanians living in Paris. And you write in your *Journal* about the "Romanian diaspora." But I think I detect a contradiction in your feeling of exile. You want to be in exile, and at the same time you don't. "To live the life of a poor student, but not necessarily that of an émigré," you write. You decided to write in French. "Imitate Dante, not Ovid," is what you had to say about that. You find something specifically Romanian in the very fact of emigration: it "is an extension of the constant movement of the Romanian shepherds with their flocks." And you also say "This myth of the Romanian diaspora gives a meaning to my exile's existence." And, just a moment ago: "For me, exile was part of the Romanian destiny." Can you clarify your feelings of that time at all?

·E·   There are two currents in the tradition of the Romanian people, two complementary spiritual expressions. One, the pastoral current, is the lyrical and philosophical expression of the shepherds. The other is that of the settled communities, the agricultural population. In Romania, up until about 1920, 80 percent of the population was made up of people who worked in agriculture, but there was also a very important minority of shepherds. These shepherds, who led their flocks to and fro between Czechoslovakia and the Sea of Azov, opened up the Romanian people to a much wider world than that of their own villages. The shepherds and their pastoral strains made the largest contribution to Romanian folk poetry. The finest Romanian ballads, especially the finest of all, *Mioritsa*, originated among the shepherds. The rest came from the culture of the peasants, the settled tillers of the soil. They too made a vast contribution, above all in the field of religious folklore and popular poetry. I am deliberately simplifying, because things were much more complicated in reality; but one can say that Romanian culture is a result of the tension between settled agriculture and transhumance or, if you like, between localism, provincialism, and universalism. And you find the same tension in our written culture. There are great Romanian writers who are traditionalist, who represent, or are an extension of, the spirituality of the villages, of the settled communities; there are others who are open to the world at large, "universalists" (they have even been accused of cosmopolitanism). One might also say that the former concerned themselves with religion, with mysticism, while the others have tended to be critical minds, drawn to science. But what matters is the creative tension between the two tendencies. The greatest Romanian poet, Eminescu, the most important Romanian writer of the nineteenth century, achieved a wonderful synthesis of the two currents.

So, to answer your question, it is true that I was cut off from the land of my birth, but that deprivation already existed in the Romanian past, as it did in the history of the Jewish people—an exemplary history, in a way, and one that I regard as one of the models for the Christian world. Speaking for the Romanians in Paris and, more generally, for all those who have decided to remain in the West, I said that we weren't émigrés but that we were in exile. I thought that an exiled writer should imitate Dante, not Ovid, because Ovid had been proscribed—and his work is one of lamentation and regrets, dominated by his nostalgia for all he had lost—whereas Dante accepted that deprivation, and more than accepted it, since it was thanks to that exemplary experience that he was able to complete *The Divine Comedy*. For Dante, exile was more than a stimulus; it was the very wellspring of his inspiration. So I said that we mustn't write nostalgically but, on the contrary, should try to profit from that profound crisis, from that separation, as Dante did in Ravenna.

·R· So, to echo Nietzsche's phrase, you have never been a man of resentment?

·E· No, I felt that the experience of exile possessed the value of an initiation. And the thing that seemed to me potentially disastrous was precisely that: resentment. It is something that paralyzes creativity and drains life of all savor. A resentful man, in my eyes, is an unhappy man, a man unable to profit from life. His life is almost without substance. That was what I was trying to say. I gave several lectures for our group and wrote many articles for the Romanian press in Paris, and western Europe generally, in which I said that we must accept the separation of exile and, above all, create. Creation is the only answer one can give to fate, to the "terror of history."

·R· Throughout your *Journal* the two most deeply ingrained and frequently recurring images seem to be the Labyrinth and Ulysses: both double figures. In Ulysses, wandering and homeland are inseparable; and the Labyrinth has no meaning unless it makes us lose our way—but not

94

into ultimate chaos and not for ever. What are your feelings about Ulysses today?

·E·   Ulysses, for me, is the prototype of man, not only modern man but the man of the future too, because he typifies the hunted traveler. His journey was a journey toward the center, searching for Ithaca—which is to say, searching for himself. He was a good navigator, but fate—in other words, the ordeals of initiation he had to go through—forced him again and again to defer his return home. I think the myth of Ulysses is very important for us all. We shall all of us turn out to be a little like Ulysses, seeking for ourselves, hoping to reach the end of our journey, and then, when we reach our home and homeland once again, no doubt discovering our selves. But, as with the Labyrinth, as with every quest, there is a danger that we may lose ourselves. If one does succeed in emerging from the Labyrinth, in finding one's way back home, then one becomes another being.

·R·   You compare Ulysses to modern man, but you also recognize yourself in him?

·E·   Yes, I recognize myself. I think that his myth constitutes an exemplary model for a certain way of existing in the world.

·R·   He could be your personal emblem?

·E·   Yes.

·R·   So, you saw a lot of your Romanian friends. That means Ionesco, Cioran, and also Voronca and Lupasco.

·E·   I knew Cioran very well. We had already been friends in Romania, between 1933 and 1938, and I was delighted to meet him again, here in Paris. I had admired Cioran ever since he published his first articles in 1932, when he was scarcely twenty-one. His knowledge of philosophy and literature was most exceptional for his age. He had already read Hegel and Nietzsche, the German mystics, and Asvagosha. Apart from that, and despite his youth, he had acquired an amazing mastery over language. He wrote not only philosophical essays but polemical pieces of extraordinary power; he stood comparison with the writers of apocalypses and the most famous political pamphleteers. His first book in Romania, *On the Heights of Despair,* was utterly gripping as a novel and at the same time melancholy and terrible, depressing and exalting. Cioran wrote in Romanian so well that you couldn't imagine it possible that one day he would display the same literary perfection in French. I think his example is unique. It's true that he had always had a great regard for style, for stylistic perfection. He used to say, quite seriously, that Flaubert was right when he toiled for a whole night just to avoid a subjunctive.

I became friends with Eugene Ionesco in Paris. I had met him earlier, in Bucharest; but, as he has jokingly pointed out to me several times, there was a difference of two years in our ages. At twenty-six I was "famous," back from India, and a university teacher, while he, Ionesco, at twenty-four, was still at work on his first book. So those "two years" made a vast difference. There was a gulf between us! But it vanished the moment we met in Paris. Eugene Ionesco was well known in Romania as a poet and, above all, as a literary critic, or rather as an "anticritic," since he had written a book—a very polemical one, called *No!*— that caused quite a commotion in Romania because it attempted to prove that literary criticism doesn't exist as an autonomous discipline. In Paris I was curious to find out what path he would decide to take: philosophical inquiry? prose literature? journal? At all events, I had no idea he was at work on *The Bald Soprano.* By the end of the first night I was already a great and sincere admirer of his theatrical talent, and I had no further doubts about his literary career in France. What I like first and foremost about Ionesco's plays is their poetic richness and symbolic power of imagination. Each one of his plays reveals an imaginary universe that partakes simultaneously of the structures of dream and the symbolism of mythology. I react above all to the dream poetry that gives his plays their structure. And yet one can't talk merely of "oneirism." It sometimes seems

to me that I am a spectator of the "great dreams" of living
Matter, of the Earth Mother, of the childhood of future
heroes and failures; and some of those "great dreams" open
out into mythology.

It was also in Paris that I met Stéphane Lupasco,
whom I regard very highly, both as a man and as a thinker.
Voronca I met only two or three times, unfortunately; as
you know, he killed himself very soon after my arrival. But
when I met him, in 1946, I asked him: "How do you manage to write poems in French?" And his answer was: "With
great agony."

·R· Mentioning Lupasco makes me think of
Bachelard, whom we didn't talk about earlier, but whom
you knew.

·E· I met him several times; the first was at Lupasco's,
as a matter of fact. He had read two of my books. He had
found *The Techniques of Yoga* very interesting, particularly
the imaginary world he had found there, in the Tantric vi-
sual meditations. He had also read my *Patterns in Comparative Religion* and found that fascinating, too. He told me he
used it a great deal in his lectures because it contained so
many images that were useful for analyzing the symbolism
of earth, water, the sun, the Earth Mother. Unfortunately, it
was only between 1948 and 1950 that we saw anything of
each other. After that I lost sight of him. But I was a great
admirer of his. And apart from that I liked his life-style. He
lived exactly like Brancusi. Great philosopher and historian
of science that he was, he still went on living his peasant
life, just like Brancusi in his studio.

·R· You've mentioned Brancusi, and earlier you were
talking about the contradictory unity of Romanian culture.
Can we take that a little further? What does being Romanian mean, ultimately? And what does it mean to you in
particular?

·E· I felt I was the descendant and heir of a culture
that was fascinating because it was a bridge between two

97

worlds: the Western, purely European world, and that of
the East. I was part of both those worlds: a Westerner, because both the Romanian language and many of our customs
are inherited from Rome; but also part of a culture influenced by the East and rooted in the Neolithic era. That is
true for any Romanian; but I'm sure it's just the same for a
Bulgarian or a Serbo-Croat, in short for all the Balkans,
southeastern Europe, and part of Russia. And this East-
West tension—traditionalism versus modernism; mysticism,
religion, and contemplation versus rationalism, the spirit of
criticism and the desire for concrete creation—this polarity
is found in all cultures. Between Dante and Petrarch, for
example, or, as Papini put it, between the poetry of stone
and the poetry of honey. Between Pascal and Montaigne,
Goethe and Nietzsche. But this creative tension is possibly
a little more complex with us, because we exist on the con-
fines of dead empires, as one French writer put it. Being
Romanian, for me, is living and expressing, and giving
value, to that way of living in the world. It's my heritage,
and it must be taken advantage of! Learning Italian, for us, is
nothing. And when I began learning Russian, the Slavic
element in the Romanian vocabulary helped me a lot. I took
advantage of those things, which were given to me simply
by the fact that I was born where I was. This very rich heritage probably hasn't yet been given its full value in literature, in the culture of the educated, but it is there in the
creative tradition of our folklore.

·R·   Perhaps this is the moment to talk about *Zalmoxis,
the Vanishing God.*

·E·   That was a very personal book as well as an experiment in method. The problem was this: we Romanians
possess a folklore tradition and also a historical tradition,
equally sizable; but the evidence, the material, is vague and
scattered. So how, on that basis, was it possible to reconstruct the beliefs of the Dacians? At the same time,
there were various other problems that fascinated me. In
the legend of Master Manole we find a human sacrifice. In
order to finish the monastery, Master Manole was obliged

98

to wall up his wife. It is a legend you find throughout the Balkans. The linguists, Balkanologists, and Romanists all agree that the Romanian version is the original. So why should this ballad in particular be a masterpiece of Romanian popular tradition? And how did it come about that the nostalgia of the nomadic shepherd and his whole *Weltanschauung* are expressed in *Mioritsa?* Faced with such problems, the historian of religions undoubtedly has a chance to see things that the pure folklore expert would miss.

·R· Would you regard Brancusi as an exemplary figure as far as "Romanianness" or "being Romanian" is concerned?

·E· Yes, in the sense that, when he came to Paris, Brancusi lived in the atmosphere of the artistic avant-garde and yet never abandoned his Carpathian peasant's style of living. He expressed his artistic thought by following models he had found in the Carpathians, but he did not simply copy those models and produce a cheapened form of folklore. He recreated them, he succeeded in inventing those archetypal shapes that dazzled the world because he delved so deeply, right down to the Neolithic tradition, and it was there that he found the roots, the wellsprings. Instead of taking his inspiration from modern Romanian folk art, he went back to the origins of that folk art.

·R· Can we say that he rediscovered, not the forms, but the forces that gave those forms their vitality?

·E· Precisely. And if he did succeed in rediscovering them, it was because he stubbornly maintained the same way of life as his parents, his kinfolk, did in the Carpathians.

·R· In your *Journal* you express regret that your shyness kept you from meeting Brancusi. We regret it too. But we do nevertheless have a literary encounter, if I may put it that way, between Brancusi and Mircea Eliade. There is a fine and insufficiently well-known piece of yours in which you elucidate—as you did just now—the deep roots of

99

Brancusi's inspiration and then go on to give a very personal and well-founded analysis of what you yourself learned from your painstaking decipherment of primordial myths. You consider the central images in Brancusi's work— ascent, the tree, the bird—and you draw this conclusion: that Brancusi made matter fly, become airborne, as the alchemist does. And he did so by a marriage of contraries, since what gives an image, a sign, the greatest degree of lightness is precisely that which is also the sign of opacity, of falling, of weight: stone. That very fine article occupies an eminent place in your work.

Homeland, the World

·R· I used to wonder: how is a man like Mircea Eliade able to reconcile such a diversity of languages, cultures, countries, houses, in his life? I begin to see the answer now; but I would like to ask you how your homeland and the world interact in your life.

·E· The homeland, for every exile, is the mother tongue he still continues to speak. Fortunately, my wife is Romanian too, and she plays the role of homeland for me, if you like, since we talk to each other in Romanian. The homeland, for me, is therefore the language I speak with her and my friends, but above all with her; and it is the language in which I dream and also write my journal. So it isn't a wholly inner homeland, not only a land of dreams. But there is no contradiction, no tension even, between the world and the homeland. Wherever one is, there is a *center of the world.* As long as you are in that center, you are at home, you are truly in the real *self* and at the center of the cosmos. Exile helps you to understand that the world is never foreign to you once you have a central stance in it. I have not merely understood this "symbolism of the center" intellectually: I live it.

·R· You have traveled a great deal, yet I feel that you aren't in fact a traveler by vocation.

·E· It's possible that the most important of my travels,

for me, were the ones I made on foot, between the ages of twelve and nineteen, in the summertime. I used to spend weeks and weeks living in villages or monasteries, impelled by a desire to leave the plain of Bucharest and explore the Carpathians, the Danube, the fishing villages on the delta, the Black Sea. I know my country very well.

·R· The final page of your *Journal* is devoted to the subject of travel. You say: "The fascination of travel derives not only from the spaces, from the forms and colors—the places one visits or passes through—but also from the various personal 'times' that one reactivates. The further I journey through life, the stronger is my impression that all journeys take place in time and space concomitantly."

·E· Yes, the fact that, when visiting Venice, for example, I am reliving the time of my first trips to Venice. One rediscovers the whole past in space: a street, a church, a tree. Suddenly time past has been regained. That is one of the things that make traveling such an enrichment of the self, of one's own experience. One finds oneself again, one can communicate with the person one was fifteen, twenty, years before. One meets him, one meets oneself, one meets one's time, one's historical moment, of twenty years ago.

·R· Might one say that you are a man of nostalgia, but of joyful nostalgia?

·E· Yes. Yes! That's very well put, and you're quite right. I rediscover precious things through such nostalgia. And in that way I feel that I never lose anything, that nothing is ever lost.

·R· I think that here we are touching on things that are very important for you: nothing is lost, and you never feel the sharp tooth of resentment.

·E· Yes, that's true.

✑ Interlude

·R· You have written very little for the theater— a play about Brancusi, *La Colonne sans fin,* and a modern *Iphigenia.* But if one is to judge by certain passages in *The Forbidden Forest* and in your *Journal* (when you speak about Artaud), you have nevertheless given particular attention to the representation of time in the theater: the representation of imaginary—mythical—time within the real duration of a theatrical performance.

·E· Yes, just as liturgical time is different from profane time—the time of clocks, of timetables—so theatrical time is an "excursion" outside ordinary time. Music as well—certain music at least, and I am thinking particularly of Bach—sometimes takes us outside everyday time. Everyone has had that experience, so it is one that can help even the most "profane" mind to understand sacred time, liturgical time. But I am just as fascinated by the condition of the actor as by this quality of theatrical time. The actor experiences a sort of "transmigration." Is embodying so many characters not the same as undergoing the same number of reincarnations? At the end of his life, I am certain the actor possesses a human experience different in quality from ours. I don't believe that one can indulge in such a process of constant reincarnation with impunity, or not without a certain ascesis.

·R· Is the actor a sort of shaman?

103

·E·   At all events, the shaman is an actor, insofar as certain of his practices are theatrical in their nature. In a more general way, shamanism can be regarded as a common root of both philosophy and the representational arts. The shamanic tales of journeys to heaven or hell lie at the root of certain epic poems and of certain tales. The shaman, in order to play his role as the community's spiritual guide, in order to edify that community, to reassure it, must at the same time represent invisible things and demonstrate his powers—even if it means using tricks. The performance he gives to that end, the masks he wears on such occasions—all that does constitute one of the sources of theater. The shamanic model may be traced even in *La Divina Commedia:* like the shaman's, Dante's ecstatic journey reestablishes for every reader what is exemplary and a worthy object of faith.

🐚 Chicago

Living in Chicago

·R·   You have been teaching at the University of Chicago now for almost twenty years. Why Chicago?

·E·   I was invited to give the famous Haskell Lectures, which had also been given by Rudolf Otto and by Massignon. Those six lectures were published under the title *Rites and Symbols of Initiation.* After the death of Joachim Wach, who had invited me to give the lectures, the dean pressed me to accept a professorship and become head of the history of religions department. I hesitated for a long while, then agreed to take the post for four years. And then I stayed on, because what I was doing was very important to me and important also for our discipline and American culture generally. In 1957 there were three chairs of the history of religions in the United States. Now there are nearly thirty, half of them filled by former students in our department. But it wasn't only the fascination of the work itself that made me stay; it was the atmosphere there at the university, the enormous freedom, the tolerance. I have not been alone in finding that atmosphere so admirable, almost like paradise! Georges Dumézil, who was invited over, Paul Ricoeur, who is now a colleague of ours—they both felt the same way. This vast freedom in the way one teaches, in the expression of one's opinions, and in one's communication with the students, whom one has plenty of time to get to know, in seminars or at one's own home or theirs . . . . One feels that one is doing something really worthwhile.

·R· You feel that you laid the foundation of a "school" of the history of religions, a trend in interpretation and research that now stretches across the entire United States?

·E· There can be no doubt that Chicago laid the foundation of our discipline's success. But that success was also due in part to the historical moment. Some Americans had realized that, in order to enter into meaningful dialogue with an African or an Indonesian, knowing all about political economy and sociology isn't enough. You need to know about their culture. And you can't understand an exotic or archaic culture unless you've come to grips with its source, which is always religious. Add to that the fact that the United States Constitution, as you know, prohibits the teaching of religion in a state university. Americans were afraid, during the nineteenth century, that a chair of "religion" would become simply a chair of Christian theology or of the history of the Christian church. Well, after the first ten or so chairs had been a success, then the other universities saw that it was the general history of religions that was involved—that we also taught Hinduism, Islam, and the primitive religions; so they too were prepared to accept such things being taught on their campuses. At first the courses were camouflaged under titles like "The Religions of Asia" or "Indian Studies," for example; but today we have departments like "The History and Phenomenology of Religions."

·R· Doesn't the historian of religions, however detached one might at first suppose him to be from current affairs—doesn't he sooner or later find himself in the same situation as his colleagues in the field of physics or geography, since, as you know better than anyone, American universities have all been through the same crisis of conscience: is it possible to collaborate in nuclear armament, in the bombing of Vietnam? For, after all, it is not absolutely out of the question that in any "psychological warfare" the manufacture of "messianic bombs" could possess a certain strike power. One has only to think of the uses to which the advertising industry puts psychological research. Isn't it possible that men of war might use a knowledge of religious myths in the same way?

·E·   Yes . . . . I wrote an article on messianism, before the independence of the Congo. I am fairly familiar with the Bantu messianic myths, and I predicted things that did happen later, after independence: they destroyed their cattle, because the mythic ancestor was about to return. Certain crimes, certain excesses, were already perfectly predictable to those who had read the relevant books on the messianism of archaic peoples. So I don't really think that the generals are about to start scouring the history of religions in search of weapons. On the other hand, I do see our discipline as having a "social function," a function that is constantly growing and even acquiring a mass appeal: it has paved the way for a certain religious ecumenism, and not only within Christianity: it has encouraged meetings between representatives of a variety of religions.

·R·   What sort of life do you lead in Chicago?

·E·   The University stands in a huge park bordering Lake Michigan, about six miles from the center of the city. Everything is concentrated there: the enormous library, and the Oriental Institute with its wonderful archives, a museum, small but very fine, and the great specialists in all the Oriental Studies. In fact . . . everything! That is a great help, not only in gaining access to the information one needs, but also in checking it. I can always consult a Hittite or Assyrian specialist or someone just back from a fieldwork trip in some particular Indian village. For someone doing research, it's much better than European universities, where the buildings and the professors are so scattered. American universities tend to be modeled on Oxford and Cambridge. I like the campus in Chicago very much.

·R·   And the city itself?

·E·   Architecturally speaking, Chicago is regarded as the world leader: apartment blocks twenty to thirty stories high. Personally I don't like them, because they're black. It's the fashion these days for all buildings to be black. I accept that all the darkened glass you see does enable people working inside to see out without being seen. But I would prefer colors that blended with the landscape.

·R·   What is your own house like?

·E·   We live up on the second floor of a small house, with a garden and a wooden balcony. It's on a very wide, rather lovely tree-lined avenue. It's only fifty feet or so from my office, where I keep part of my library, quite often work during the day, and see my students. The university library is about a quarter of a mile away, and the classrooms about half a mile. Everyone lives in the same small area, which I like. It's a beautiful district, and we're very happy there, because there are always squirrels that come to beg for nuts. In winter we have a cardinal—you know, the beautiful red bird that we unfortunately don't have in Europe. It's a creature that poses quite a problem, and I'm amazed that theologians haven't lighted on it as an example to illustrate the workings of Providence. Because what other explanation can there be of how such a very flamboyantly red bird has survived? There is no way it can camouflage itself. Even when it's up in a tree, you can see it from miles away. I'm joking, but it is a puzzle all the same.

·R·   Is where you live important to you?

·E·   Yes, I really can't live in a house, or even a room, that I don't like. I was oppressed in that way in both London and Oxford. I can't live just anywhere. There must be something about a place that pleases me, attracts me, so that I feel at home. I looked hard for a house I felt I could really live in.

I'm not very fond of America's "wide open spaces" as such. I like the campus and certain other things about Chicago, such as the vast feeling of power you get in its center. I'm very fond of certain cities like San Francisco, Boston, parts of New York, and Washington. I like certain places like Santa Barbara, San Francisco Bay; but it isn't a country like Italy, like France, where the landscape is im-

mensely beautiful, where it has a long history and variety.
Chicago stands in the middle of a plain that stretches for
hundreds and hundreds of miles; every now and then there
is a city and wealthy residential neighborhoods, rather like
artificial Gardens of Eden—beautiful houses, but people
just shut themselves away in them, and it's all rather artificial. And even in the most beautiful American cities some
neighborhoods are appallingly ugly. My attitude toward the
wide open spaces, or the American way of life, some aspects
of which I find fascinating, is not a negative one, but I remain a European. What I like about America, to take one
example, is the importance given to the wife, and not just
from the social point of view but the cultural and spiritual
point of view as well. People always invite you with your
wife. When they wanted me to stay in the United States, the
first thing they asked me was whether my wife liked it there.
The attention paid to the wife, the family, that's something I
like very much. And after all, the Americans are quite
justifiably accused of a great many things, but there are a lot
of admirable things about them that are seldom mentioned:
for example, their extremely tolerant attitude in religious
and spiritual matters.

Teacher or Guru?

·R·   Essentially, then, America is where you work. I
would like to know what kind of teacher you are.

·E·   I have never been a "systematic" teacher. In
Bucharest, even in my early days, I took it for granted that
the students had already read a life of Buddha, some of the
Upanishads, something about the problem of evil. I didn't
begin in a didactic way, and I didn't prepare too much in
advance—I never wrote out my lectures. I would have a few
notes, then watch how the students reacted. Today it's much
the same. I make a plan, I sit quietly for a few hours before
the lesson and think about it, I pick my quotations, but I
don't write anything out. There's no great risk attached: if I
repeat myself, well that's not so very serious; and if I forget
something, then I talk about it next day or at the end of the

class. The American system is excellent: after the fifty minutes of lecture time, there is always ten minutes for discussion, for questions. Things were totally different in my student days: the professor appeared, spoke, then vanished; you didn't set eyes on him again for another week. Perhaps things have changed everywhere, though. At any rate, it sometimes happens during those ten minutes of conversation that a question makes me realize I've left out some important detail. Paul Ricoeur is amazed at the relationship we have with our students in Chicago. At Nanterre he sometimes had a thousand students; there was no way of knowing any of them, he was teaching philosophy to a faceless crowd. In Chicago the relationship is personal. In your very first class you say to the students: "Write your names on this sheet of paper, then come and see me." At the beginning of each year I keep two whole afternoons a week free so as to meet them all, half an hour each—even the second-year students, to refresh my memory: to ask what they did during the vacation, what they want to do now. And then, a month into the term, I see them all again, this time for an hour. To be frank, I find giving lectures to a hundred or so students less and less enjoyable. There was a time, in Romania especially, when I was talking about things that almost no one knew about, so there was a thrill in it. I was using my own language, I was talking to the young, and I was young myself. I still had so many things to say, so many things to find out—things that by now I've mostly written down, published. After all that activity, forty years or so of it, I naturally feel that I have less to say as a lecturer. But what I still love is the seminar, where one can work together with the students. My seminar in 1976, for example, dealt with alchemy and hermetism in the Renaissance. That was exciting. That's what I like: really getting down to the details of a subject with a small group who know their stuff, really digging into certain problems that are close to my heart. And that's when the student learns how to work, when he learns what method means. He writes an essay, we listen to it, I invite the other students to make their comments, I make some of my own, and we go on talking like that,

110

sometimes for hours on end. But I feel I'm not wasting my time, because what I'm giving them is something they could never find just in books. And the first-semester interviews I have with them are irreplaceable in just the same way.

·R· However, you do manage to live a life of your own as well? Your life as a writer and researcher?

·E· Yes, because the system contains a break in classes, a period for the student to do his reading. So in the winter quarter I hold only one seminar. That means that I can get on with my own work. But of course, when I feel I can be of help to someone, then I'm glad to leave off my own work, or I work a little longer in the evening or start earlier in the morning. I make an effort. Because I feel it's important. If there's someone who listens but doesn't seem all that interested, then I suggest a few books he could read— mine or someone else's.

·R· Finally, are you a teacher or a guru?

·E· There is always the danger in America, particularly on the West Coast, in certain cases at least, that one is going to be taken for a guru. One year when I was teaching a course at the University of Santa Barbara on Indian religions, from the *Rig Veda* to the *Bhagavad Gītā,* the students used to come to me after class as though I were a guru who could solve all their private probems. I said to them: "Don't confuse one thing with another. Here, I am a teacher, not a guru. I can certainly help you, but as a teacher. What I am trying to do here is to present things to you as I think they are."

The Youth of America

·R· These young Americans, whom you know at first hand, and for whom, sometimes, religion is not simply something to be studied, how do you see them, and what is happening to them now?

·E· What I saw in Chicago, and in Santa Barbara as well, was most exciting. In America, the history of religions

111

is a fashionable discipline at the moment, not just among students, who, as Maritain said, are "illiterate from the religious point of view," but also with a lot of people who are simply curious to find out about other people's religions: Hinduism, Buddhism, and all the archaic and primitive religions. Shamanism has become almost a craze. It has caught the interest of painters, of theatrical directors, and a great many young people: they think that their drugs are going to help them understand the shaman's experiences. Some of these students have found their absolute in ephemeral sects, such as those of Meher Baba, Hari Krishna, the Jesus Freaks, and certain "Zen" sects. I don't encourage them, but I don't criticize their choice either, because they say to me: "Before, I was always on some drug or other the whole time, just a hollow shell; there was nothing I believed in, I'd made two suicide attempts, I almost got killed one day when I was totally stoned, and now I've found the *absolute!*" I don't tell them that this "absolute" of theirs isn't exactly of the finest quality, because, for the moment, this young man who has been existing in chaos, in a state of pure nihilism and dangerous aggression toward the community—well, he has at least found something. And it is on the foundation of that "absolute" of his, which is often a pseudo-absolute, that he may rediscover himself, that he may go on later to read the Upanishads, Meister Eckhart, or the Kabbala and start searching for a personal truth. I have rarely encountered a student who has successfully made a direct transition from a religious void, from a state of almost neurotic instability, to a clearly articulated religious position, whether Christian, Judaic, Buddhist, or Islamic. No, they always go through a sort of pseudomorphosis, something easy, showy, rather spurious, at least to outside eyes, since for the young people themselves it is the absolute, it is salvation. Then there is a second stage, when they move on to a more balanced, more meaningful form of belief.

·R·   You told me the other day that the repudiation of monotheism, and of its obverse, atheism, takes one of two forms among these young people: either that of "natural religion," "cosmic religion," or else that of "Eastern religions."

·E· Yes, it begins as an almost instinctive reaction against the "Establishment" and therefore against their parents. Their parents attend the synagogue or the church, Protestant or Catholic; so they reject that religion, that particular religious tradition, completely. They refuse to take any interest in it whatever. It's impossible to get them to read a single word about it. One day a Jewish student came to see me; Judaism is meaningless, he told me, it's a fossil. Whereas he had just found revelation in a guru, a yogin who had been in town only a few weeks. I asked him: "What do you know about Judaism?" He knew nothing, he hadn't read a single psalm, a single prophet, nothing. The Kabbala I won't even mention. So I tried to persuade him that he should. "Read some of the texts of your own religious tradition," I told him, "then you can either build on that or ignore it." No, he didn't want to. It was meaningless. You see, that's exactly the attitude of a younger generation when it is rejecting everything wholesale: the system, their parents' values and way of life, their religious tradition. And so, for a certain section of these young people, in rebellion against everything, Far Eastern forms of gnosis, and especially "Yoga" and "Zen," have an extraordinary power of fascination. I'm sure it does them some good. When a Ramakrishna mission arrives, there is always some swami who helps them to read certain books. And sometimes they don't remain content just to read works on shamanism among the American Indians; they go and spend part of their vacations among this or that tribe.

What is happening to young Americans now? I can't answer that. In the universities, everyone says that drugs have lost a great deal of their attraction. "Meditation" is the up-and-coming thing at the moment—all kinds of meditation, though "transcendental meditation" is certainly the most widespread. I think that these techniques are tools that may help them, in the early stages; later they will find masters who will guide them toward ways of achieving a more articulated realization. And even if they abandon their "California" experience and become civil servants, taxi-drivers, teachers, I am sure they will have been enriched by it.

The Future of the Gods

·R· The press is only too eager to give coverage to sects and schisms. Yesterday it was Manson and Moon. Today, in France, it is the battle of the Intégristes. I would like to know what you think about these "religious news stories" and also about the hippie movement, which you know at first hand.

·E· As far as the Roman Catholic Church is concerned, it is quite clear that the present crisis is not merely a crisis of authority but one of very old liturgical and theological structures. I don't believe it means the end of the church as a whole, but possibly it means the end of a certain form of Christian church. It seems to me that this crisis is bound to be creative and that once the trials and controversies are over, other, more interesting, more living, more meaningful things may emerge. But one cannot see into the future. As for the sects: as always, these movements stand a great chance of revealing something new, something positive. But it is the hippie phenomenon that seems to me the most important, because it has given us proof that a younger generation—the descendants of ten generations of Christians, whether Protestant or Roman Catholic—has rediscovered the religious dimension of cosmic life, of nakedness, of sexuality. And on this point I have to take issue with those who regard the hippies' leaning toward sexuality and the orgy as merely part of the worldwide movement toward sexual permissiveness. In their case, what is involved above all else is what one might call "Edenic nudity," and the sexual act is seen as a form of ritual. They have rediscovered the deeply religious meaning of life, and by that experience they have freed themselves from all sorts of religious, philosophical, and sociological superstitions. They are free. They have rediscovered the dimension of cosmic sacrality, the experience of which was abolished from our society a very long time ago, as early as Old Testament days. You remember how the biblical prophets clamored in indignation and grief against the worship of Baal and Belit, which was in fact a worship based on a cosmically structured religion of immense stature. It was a religion that manifested the world's sacrality through a goddess, through hierogamy, through the orgy. Those religious experiences were devalued by Mosaic monotheism, and particularly by the prophets. After Moses and the prophets, any return to a cosmic type of religiosity had become meaningless. Well, in America we have seen the rediscovery of a religious experience that had been supposed totally outdated in its collective "religious" aspect, even though the hippies didn't ever refer to it as that. They tried, with the energy of despair, to rediscover the sacrality of life as a whole. It was a reaction against the meaninglessness of urban living, against that desacralization of the world that occurs in American cities. They were unable to understand the religious value of an organized church—for them, that was "The Establishment"—but they did discover this other thing, and they were saved. They rediscovered the sacred wellsprings of life, the religious importance of life.

·R·   What do you see in the future as far as religion is concerned? Is your view at all like that of Malraux, who said, more or less, that "the twenty-first century will be religious or it will not be?"

·E·   One can't predict anything. The freedom of the human spirit is such that one cannot foretell what it will do. If I spoke of the hippie movement just now, it was also because it is an example of our inexhaustible and unpredictable creativity. Perhaps that movement will disappear, if it hasn't already; perhaps it will become totally politicized or, on the contrary, cease to have the slightest importance. What is certain, however, is that unexpected developments do occur from time to time.

     What makes it even more difficult to predict anything at all in this area is that certain "religious" forms

115

can easily fail to be recognized as such. A creation can be so new that in its early stages, and even for centuries, it isn't regarded as religious at all. For example, it is possible that certain movements, apparently political on the surface, are coming into being now or are already expressing the desire for a certain profound liberty; such movements could be transpolitical, or could become so, but not be recognized as such because of the newness of their language. Think of Christianity. In Rome, the Christians were accused of being atheists because they refused to go into the temples and do homage to the gods by making sacrifices to them. They were rejecting the Establishment! The Romans were quite happy to let you worship any god you chose: Sarapis or Yahweh, Attis or Jupiter, they didn't mind. But whatever your gods, they had to be venerated. And the Christians refused to venerate them, so they were branded as atheists. It was Christian atheism! All because no one recognized the *religious* value of their behavior.

One can't predict anything. But I believe that certain primordial revelations can never disappear. Even in the most technological civilizations there are elements that cannot change, because there will always be day and night, summer and winter. Even in a city without trees, there is still the sky with its stars, one can still look up and see the moon and stars. As long as we still have night and day, summer and winter, I don't think man can be changed. Whether we will or no, we are part of that cosmic rhythm. One can change values. The religious values of the agricultural community—summer, night, seed—are no longer ours; yet that rhythm still remains: light and dark, night and day. Even the most areligious person alive still exists within that cosmic rhythm; he experiences it in his own individual existence: in his daytime life, then in sleep and dreams—and he does still have dreams. Of course, we are conditioned by our economic and social structures, and the expressions of our religious experience are always conditioned by our language, by society, by our interests. But, nevertheless, we still assume that human condition here—here in this cosmos, whose rhythms and cycles are ineluctably given. So we assume our human condition on the basis of that fundamental existential condition. And that "basic" human being—it is permissible to call him "religious," whatever appearances may seem to say, because we are talking about the meaning of life. What I am sure of is that any future forms of religious experience will be quite different from those we are familiar with in Christianity, Judaism, or Islam, all of which are fossilized, outmoded, drained of meaning. I am sure that new forms, new expressions, will come. What will they be? I cannot say. The great surprise is always the freedom of the human spirit, its creativity.

History and Hermeneutics

The Giddy Heights of Knowledge

·R· "I have spent thirty years and more now among exotic, barbaric, indomitable gods and goddesses, nourished on myths, obsessed by symbols, held in the spell of so many images swimming back up to me from worlds long submerged beneath time past. Those thirty years now appear to me as so many stages in a long initiation. Each of those divine forms, those myths or symbols, represents a danger confronted and overcome. How many times have I just escaped 'losing' myself—losing my way in that labyrinth where I was in danger of being killed, sterilized, 'emasculated' (by one of those terrible mother goddesses, for example). An infinite series of intellectual adventures—and I use that word 'adventure' in its primary sense of an existential risk. They were not, all those things, mere items of 'knowledge,' acquired piecemeal and at leisure from books; they were so many encounters, confrontations, and temptations. I am perfectly aware, now, of all the perils that I skirted during that long 'quest': first and foremost, the danger of forgetting that I had a goal, that I was directing my footsteps toward something, that I was trying to reach a 'center.'"

You wrote those words in your journal on 10 November 1959. There is still something slightly veiled, something sibylline about them, however. Is it possible for you to speak more clearly now?

·E· The mind is always in jeopardy when it attempts to

119

penetrate the deeper meaning of such mythological or religious creations, each of which is an existential expression of man in the world. Of man: of a primitive hunter, of a Far Eastern peasant, of a fisherman in the Pacific. In the hermeneutic striving of the historian of religions and the phenomenologist to understand the situation of that man *from within,* there is a risk: not merely of fragmenting himself, but also of becoming spellbound by the shaman's magic, the yogin's powers, the exaltation of some member of an orgiastic society. I don't say that one is tempted to *become* the yogin or the shaman or the warrior or the ecstatic. But one does feel oneself being taken over by existential situations that are alien to the Westerner and perilous for him. This confrontation with exotic forms, which can come to obsess you, tempt you, is a danger of a psychic order. That is why I compared that quest to a long journey through a labyrinth, because it is a sort of initiation ordeal. The effort necessary to understand cannibalism, for example: it was not by instinct that man became a cannibal, it was as the result of a theology and a mythology. And the historian of religions, if he wants to understand, is obliged to relive that situation and all the rest of man's infinite series of existential positions in the world.

When man became conscious of his mode of being in the world and of the responsibilities linked with it, a decision was taken, a tragic decision. I am thinking here of the discovery of agriculture—not the cultivation of cereal crops in the Near East but that of tubers in the tropics. The notion these people arrived at was that the food plant in question was the result of a primordial murder. A divine being had been killed, then cut up, and the pieces of his body had given birth to plants not known before, in particular the tuberous plants that thereafter provided man's main source of nourishment. But, in order to guarantee a further crop, the first murder must be ritually repeated. Hence human sacrifice, cannibalism, and other sometimes very cruel rites. Man did not merely learn that his condition required him to kill in order to live; he also took on responsibility for the vegetable kingdom, for its perenniality, and to that end he also took human sacrifice and cannibalism upon himself. This tragic concept, that life must be perpetuated by murder, was characteristic of a large proportion of humankind for thousands of years; and when one wishes, not simply to describe it as an anthropologist does, but to understand it existentially, then one is committing oneself to an experience that is likewise tragic. The historian and phenomenologist of religions does not confront these myths and rituals as external objects, like an inscription to be deciphered, an institution to be analyzed. In order to understand that world from within, he must live it. He is like an actor assuming his roles, embodying them. Sometimes the gulf between that archaic world and our everyday world is so great that one's very personality can be at stake.

·R· So one has to hold on to one's own identity and also maintain one's reason against the terrible forces of the irrational?

·E· That is accurately put. We know, for example—and even the Freudians say this—that the psychiatrist is putting his own sanity in jeopardy by his constant contact with mental illness. The same goes for the historian of religions. What he studies has an effect upon him, a deep one. Religious phenomena express existential situations. You participate in the phenomenon you are attempting to decipher, as though you were poring over a palimpsest of your own genealogy and the past history of your own self. It is *your* history. And the power of the irrational is certainly lurking there. The historian of religions is motivated by an ambition to know, and therefore also to understand, the roots of his culture, of his being. At the cost of a protracted effort of anamnesis he must eventually succeed in recalling his own history—that is to say, the history of the human mind. Through that anamnesis the historian of religions is in a way recreating the *phenomenology of the mind.* But Hegel dealt with no more than two or three cultures, whereas the historian of religions is obliged to study and understand the history of the mind in its totality, from Paleolithic man onward. So he is involved in a truly universal history of mind. I believe that the

121

historian of religions perceives more clearly than researchers in other fields the continuity of the various stages of human mental development and, ultimately, the profound, fundamental unity of the mind. It is the human condition itself that is revealed in that process. It is in that sense, you understand, that the contribution made by the historian of religions seems to me crucial. It lays bare the unity of the human condition, and it does so in our modern world, which is becoming a "planetary" one.

·R·   You spoke of *temptations*. But if we think of the "temptations" of Saint Anthony as painted by Bosch, for instance, they are odd "temptations," since the objects of temptation depicted don't look in the least "tempting" to us; on the contrary, some of them are the most frightful apparitions. In what sense do you mean that you were "tempted" during your anamnesis as a historian of religions?

·E·   When you grasp the coherence, and even the nobility, the beauty, of the mythology and, let us say, the theology that provides the basis of cannibalism—when you have grasped that it is not a piece of animal behavior you are dealing with but a human act, that it is man, man as a being free to take a decision in the world, who has decided to kill and eat his fellow man—well, unconsciously, the mind is tempted by the enormous freedom it has uncovered: so one can kill, be a cannibal, without losing "human dignity." The same is true when you study the orgiastic rituals and grasp their amazing coherence: the orgy begins, and all the rules are swept away; incest and aggression are licit, and all values have been stood on their heads. And the meaning of that ritual is that it regenerates the world. When you make that discovery, then, like Nietzsche discovering his Eternal Return, you may give a shout of joy! Because there again, what you have is an invitation to total freedom. You say to yourself: what extraordinary freedom one might gain, and what creativity as a result of such liberations! Exactly like the Indonesian tribe, after its great orgy to mark the end of the year, when it has recreated a regenerated, energy-filled world. And the meaning of that for me, a Westerner, a modern man, is that I too can always begin my life again and thereby ensure a continued creativity. That is the sense in which one can talk about *temptations.*

There are also more Lucifer-like dangers, however. When you understand that a man believes he can change the world as a result of meditation and specific rituals, and when you try to find out why he is so certain that, after performing that ritual, he really will become master of the world or at least of his village—well, there again it is the temptation of absolute liberty; in other words, the suppression of the human condition. Man is a limited, conditioned being. But the freedom of a god, or a mythic ancestor, or a spirit no longer trammeled by a mortal body! Those are *temptations* certainly. But I don't want to give the impression that a historian of religions is actually tempted to become a cannibal, or take part in orgies, or commit incest!

·R·   You have mentioned both cannibalism and incest. But you have concentrated particularly on cannibalism. Is that because you see it as the tragic key to the human condition?

·E·   Incest, the temporary abolition of all laws, is a phenomenon one meets in many cultures that have no notion of cannibalism. Cannibalism, and the decision to ensure fertility or even the continued existence of the world by human sacrifice, can be regarded as an extreme situation, in my opinion.

·R·   Listening to you just now, I thought of Pasolini, whose work is haunted by the idea of the cannibalistic banquet. A banquet that in *Porcheria* (*Pigsty*) signifies that Last Supper.

·E·   Pasolini was fascinated by the problem of a regression, not to animal savagery, but to an earlier cultural phase. Cannibalism has no real importance unless it is a ritual act, unless it is integrated into the social framework. Besides, it is natural that a Christian reflecting on the meaning of the sacraments should eventually think to himself: I too am a cannibal. Another Italian, Papini—in his *Diary,* I believe—noted that the Roman Catholic Mass is not the commemoration but the reenactment of a human sacrifice, an act of homicide, and that it is followed by cannibalism: those involved are once again killing the man-king and then eating him and drinking his blood.

·R· Does the descent into the religious underworld not sometimes provoke the opposite kind of temptation in the historian of religions: a hatred for all gods, a hatred of religion itself? I am thinking of Lucretius, of Epicurus discovering the lie represented by the gods and the horror of the divine weighing down on man.

·E· It does indeed, yes. Certain historians who begin with an admiration for things religious do react in a frightening way. But you mentioned Lucretius. He was dealing with the decadent, fossilized forms of a religious universe. The gods had lost their sacred energy. That wonderful polytheistic structure had become drained of meaning. The gods were regarded as mere allegories or as the transfigured memory of early kings. It was an era of skepticism, when people could see only the horrible aspect of the gods. When one grasps things as a whole and digs down to the roots of this decision to kill, then it is another truth that emerges: man's tragic condition. Set in the whole of which they are a part, these terrible, grotesque, revolting things recover their original significance, which was to provide a meaning for life that would incorporate the unavoidable fact that any life necessarily implies the death of others—that one is doomed to kill in order to live. They express the condition imposed on the human mind and spirit by history, a tragic condition, true, but very creative, too! Confrontation with the void, with nothingness, with the demonic, the inhuman, the temptation to regress into the animal world—all those extreme and dramatic experiences are the source of man's greatest spiritual creations. Because, given those terrifying conditions, man was still able to say yes to life and find a meaning in his existence.

·R· In your *Journal* you refer to the "terrible mother goddesses." They are not a very familiar concept to us.

124

·E·   I was thinking particularly of Durga, a bloodthirsty Indian goddess, or of Kāli. They are both mother goddesses who, among other things, express the enigma at the heart of life and the universe, which is the fact that no life can perpetuate itself without risking death. These terrible goddesses demand the blood, the virility, the will, of their worshipers. But to understand them is at the same time to receive a revelation of a philosophic kind. One understands that this conjunction of virtues and sins, of crimes and generosity, of creativity and destructiveness, is the great enigma of life itself. If we are to live the existence of a man, not that of a robot or an animal or an angel, then that is precisely the reality we have to face. Moving to more familiar ground, in Yahweh, too, we find the benevolent creator combined with another, terrible, destructive, and jealous god, and that negative aspect of divinity makes it plain to us that God is *Everything.* In the same way, for all those peoples who accept the Great Mother, worship of these terrible goddesses is an introduction to the enigma of existence and life. Life itself is in fact this "terrible Great Mother" who chops off heads but also gives birth, who produces both fertility and crime and more: inspiration, generosity, wealth. This conjunction of contraries is as clearly visible in the myths of the Great Goddess as in the wrath of Yahweh in the Old Testament. And one asks oneself how a god can behave in such a way. But the lesson given by these myths and cults of the vengeful goddess or the vengeful god is that reality, life, the cosmos, *is like that.* Crime and generosity, crime and fertility. The Mother Goddess is both she who gives birth and she who slays. We don't live in a world of angels or spirits or in a purely animal world, either. We are "between." And I believe that confronting the revelation of this mystery always leads to an act of creation. I believe that the human spirit is at its most creative when faced with great ordeals.

·R·   So how does one protect oneself, mentally and spiritually, from these perils you have outlined? How does one keep to the path and avoid getting lost?

·E·   It is possible to survive as long as one is careful to

125

study not just cannibalism but also, for example, mystical experience. Then one realizes that the meaning of all that horror is that it reveals one part of the divine whole, the enigmatic whole—in other words, the coincidence of opposites in life. One comes to understand the meaning of such religious behavior, and one also comes to realize that it is only one of the ways in which the human spirit expresses itself: in his long and dramatic history, man decided at one point also to do *that*. But we also know that there were other, different decisions: mysticism, Yoga, contemplation. What shields the mind of the historian of religions—who is condemned, in a way, to work on these frightening facts—is the conviction that such terrible things do not represent the sum total, or the perfect expression, of religious experience but simply one side of it, the negative side.

The "Terror of History"

·R·   We have talked about the profound forms of cruelty to be found in archaic man and traditional religions. But what about those found in modern historical movements, which appear as so many triumphs of death? How does a historian of religions like yourself regard the terrible myths of modern man?

·E·   The historian of religions is faced with the terrible phenomenon of the desacralization of a ritual, a mystery, or a myth in which murder once had a religious meaning. It is a regression to a stage we moved out of thousands of years ago. But this "regression" doesn't even rediscover the spiritual significance that was once there; the transcendent values are now absent. The horror is multiplied, and the collective slaughter is also rendered "useless," by the fact that it no longer has any meaning. That is why such a hell is a true hell: its cruelty is a pure and absurd cruelty. When sacrificial or demonic myths or rituals are desacralized, the demonic content of their meaning is increased to a staggering extent, and all that is left is pure demonism, cruelty, and absolute crime.

·R·   I am still rather bothered by the problem, all the same, so I shall play the devil's advocate in an attempt to get

126

things clear. Might one not say that it is sacrifice that creates the sacred and gives it meaning? We can find no justification for Hitlerian murder, for the madness of Nazism. And fields full of war graves, once the years have passed and the patriotic fervor is fading, can begin to seem like the dismal end-product of an illusion. And yet, those soldiers died and killed with faith in their hearts, perhaps with exaltation. The kamikazes were allies of the Nazis, and their name means "wind of heaven." What criterion enables us to decide that the Aztecs lived out a justified illusion whereas the Nazi Storm Troopers didn't? What is the difference between ordinary murder and sacred murder?

·E· For the Aztecs, the meaning of human sacrifice lay in their belief that the victims fed and gave strength to the sun god and to the gods generally. For the SS, the annihilation of millions of people in the concentration camps also had a meaning, and even an eschatological one. They believed that they represented Good versus Evil. The same is true of the Japanese suicide pilot. We know what Good was for Nazism: fair-haired, Nordic man, what they called the pure Aryan. And the rest were incarnations of Evil, of the devil. It was almost a form of Manicheanism: the struggle of Good against Evil. In its early, Iranian, form, such dualism meant that every member of the faithful who killed a toad, a serpent, or some other creature of the devil was contributing to the purification of the world and the triumph of Good. It is possible to imagine how those sick men, or zealots, or fanatics—those modern Manicheans—saw Evil as being embodied in certain races: the Jews, the Gypsies. Sacrificing them by the millions was thus not a crime, since they were the incarnation of Evil, of the devil. Exactly the same can be said about the Gulags and the apocalyptic eschatology of the great Communist "liberation": it sees itself as confronted by enemies that represent Evil, that constitute an obstacle to the triumph of Good, the triumph of liberty, of man, and so on. All that can be compared with the Aztecs: both believed themselves to be justified. The Aztecs believed they were helping the sun god; the Nazis believed they were realizing their historical destiny. And the same is true for the Russians.

127

·R· You have often spoken about the "terror of history."

·E· The "terror of history," for me, is the feeling experienced by a man who is no longer religious, who therefore has no hope of finding any ultimate meaning in the drama of history, and who must undergo the crimes of history without grasping the meaning of them. An Israelite captive in Babylon suffered a great deal, but that suffering had a meaning: Yahweh wished to punish his people. And the captive knew that Yahweh, and therefore the Good, must ultimately triumph. For Hegel, every event, every trial, was still a manifestation of the universal Spirit and therefore had a meaning. It was possible, if not to justify, then at least to give a rational explanation of historical evil. But now historical events have been emptied of all transhistorical significance, and if they have ceased to be what they once were for the traditional world—trials inflicted on a people or an individual—then we are dealing with what I have called the "terror of history."

Hermeneutics

·R· The question of the risks run by the historian of religions brings us to the question of meaning: the meaning of religion for the believer and the meaning religious experience may have for the historian. One of the essential points of your thinking is that the historian of religions cannot avoid being a hermeneut. You also say that hermeneutics must be creative.

·E· Hermeneutics is the search for the meaning, or the meanings, that any given religious idea or phenomenon has possessed in time. One can establish the history of the various forms of religious expression, but hermeneutics means delving deeper and deeper into the meaning of those expressions. I call it creative for two reasons. First, it is creative for the hermeneut himself. The effort he makes to decipher the revelation present in any religious creation—ritual, symbol, myth, divine figure—in order to grasp its meaning, its function, its goal, that effort enriches the mind and life of the person making it in the most extraordinary way. It is an experience that the literary historian, for example, can never have. To grasp the meaning of Sanskrit poetry, to read Kalidasa, is a great discovery for an inquiring mind educated in the West: a new horizon of aesthetic values is opened up for him. But that is not as deep an experience—existentially deep—as the decipherment and comprehension of an Eastern or archaic form of religious behavior.

Hermeneutics is creative in a second sense: it reveals certain values that are not apparent on the level of immediate experience. Take the example of the cosmic tree, whether in Indonesia, Siberia, or Mesopotamia. There are certain features common to all three symbolic systems, but obviously that kinship would not be perceptible to the Mesopotamian, the Indonesian, or the Siberian. The work of hermeneutics reveals the latent significance of symbols and their continuous development. Look at the values that Christian theologians have added to the pre-Christian values of the cosmic tree, the *axis mundi,* or the cross or look, again, at the symbolism of baptism. Water has always had the meaning of baptismal "purification" all over the world. But with Christianity another value was added to that symbolism, without destroying its structure. On the contrary, it completed it, enriched it. In practice, baptism for the Christian is a sacrament because it was instituted by Christ.

Hermeneutics is also creative in yet another sense. The reader who grasps the symbolism of the cosmic tree, for example—and I know that this is true even for people not ordinarily interested in the history of religions—feels more than just an intellectual joy. He is making a discovery that is important for his whole life. From that point on, when he looks at certain trees, he will see them as an expression of the mystery of the cosmic rhythm. He will see the mystery of life reconstituting itself and continuing: winter—the loss of leaves; spring . . . . That has an importance of a quite different order from that of deciphering a Greek or Roman inscription. A discovery in the historical field is never negligible, needless to say. But in hermeneutics one is discovering a certain stance of the human spirit in the world. And, even if it isn't your own stance, it still affects you. And such encounters are undoubtedly a source of creativity. Think of the impact Japanese painting had on us in the nineteenth century, or African sculpture and masks in this century. Those weren't mere cultural discoveries; they were creative encounters.

·R· The task of hermeneutics is the acquisition of knowledge. But what is its criterion of truth? It seems to me, listening to you now, that although it is founded on "objective" scientific work, hermeneutics itself no longer requires "objective" criteria—which would imply that the subject is absent from what he is investigating—but rather criteria derived from a "poetic" truth. What we know, we change by the very act of knowing it; and we are ourselves changed by our knowledge. A hermeneutics without end, since even as we read Eliade, we are interpreting him, just as he himself is interpreting some Iranian symbol.

·E· That may be so. But when it is a question of the great symbols—the cosmic tree, for example—that link cosmic life with human existence in its cycle of death and rebirth, then there is something fundamental involved, something that will recur in different cultures: a secret of the universe that is also the secret of the human condition. And not only will we find the interdependence of the human condition and the cosmic condition revealed, but also the fact that it is a matter, for each individual, of his own destiny. That revelation may affect my own individual life.

So there is a fundamental meaning, and it is to that fundamental meaning that other meanings will be attached. When the cosmic tree acquires the meaning embodied in the Cross, that meaning is not immediately obvious to an Indonesian. But if you explain to him that to Christians this symbol signifies a regeneration, a new life, the Indonesian won't be particularly surprised; he will recognize something familiar in it. Tree or Cross, it is the same mystery of death and resurrection that is involved. The symbol is always open. And I must not forget that my interpretation is itself that of an investigator rooted in today. The interpretation is never finished.

130

·R·   You are asking us to grasp the universality of the symbol beyond the diversity of its symbolizations. You stress the indefinite openness of both the symbol and its interpretation. Yet you reject the path that would lead to a kind of relativism, a subjectivism, and, before long, to nihilism—the path that would consist in saying: "Yes, things have meaning, but the meaning is based solely on what in myself is most fortuitous and fleeting." My question now is this: does religious experience attain any transhistorical truth, and how? What "transcendence" do you recognize? Is the truth, for you, on the side of Claudel and his exegetic attitude, or on that of the existentialist, of Sartre when he said: "Man cannot do without meaning, but he invents that meaning in an empty sky"?

·E·   Certainly not on the side of that second interpretation: "in an empty sky"! It seems to me that the messages emanating from the fundamental symbols reveal a world of meanings that is not reducible simply to our historical and immanent experience. "An empty sky . . . ." It is an admirable metaphor, very expressive for a modern man whose ancestors believed that sky to be peopled with anthropomorphic beings, the gods; and of course the sky is indeed empty of such beings. I believe, for my part, that what religions reveal, and also the philosophies inspired by them—I am thinking of the Upanishads and Buddhism, of Dante, and Taoism—does touch on something essential that we are able to assimilate. Of course, it isn't something that can be learned by heart, like the latest scientific or archeological discovery. This is a purely personal statement, mark you, and I am not presenting it as the philosophical consequence of my work as a historian of religions. But at all events, the answer given by Sartre and the existentialists is not one that suits me: that "empty sky." I feel more drawn toward the "Princeton gnosis," for example. It is a striking thing to find the greatest mathematicians and astronomers of our day, men who have grown up in a wholly desacralized society, reaching scientific, even philosophic, conclusions very close to certain religious philosophies. It is striking to see physicists, and specialists in theoretical physics, reconstructing a universe in which God has his place, and also the idea of a cosmogony, of Creation. It is not unlike Mosaic monotheism, but without any anthropomorphism. It also leads back to certain Indian philosophies, of which those scientists had absolutely no inkling. It is something very important. And the significance of this "Princeton gnosis" seems to me to be confirmed by the huge success, the vast readership that Ruyer's book, *La Gnose de Princeton,* has achieved.

·R·   I should like to put my earlier question again in a more precise form. How does one reconcile a scientific attitude with a religious attitude? On the one hand, we are inclined to believe that there is something beyond the perceptible world—if not God or gods, then something divine, a spiritual world. And hermeneutics, you say, can guide us toward a way of incorporating ourselves into that divinity. On the other hand, we know, for example, that the transition from the Paleolithic to the Neolithic entailed the construction of a whole new set of beliefs, myths, and rituals. So how are we to believe, given the evidence provided by this historical, "materialist," science, that those beliefs, linked as they are to technical, economic, and social changes, can contain a transhistorical meaning, a transcendence?

·E·   I made the decision long ago to maintain a kind of discreet silence as to what I personally believe or don't believe. But I have striven all my life to understand those who do believe in particular things: the shaman, the yogin, and the Australian aborigine as well as the great saints—a Meister Eckhart or a Saint Francis of Assisi. So I shall answer your question as a historian of religions. Man being what he is, which is to say neither a spirit nor an angel, it is obvious that any experience of the sacred occurs for him within the context of a particular body, a particular mentality, a particular social environment. The primitive hunter could not apprehend the holiness and mystery of the earth's fertility as the farmer came to do later. The dividing line between those two sets of religious values is clear cut. Before it, the hunted animal's bones had a sacred significance; after it, religious values

132

were centered above all on man and woman, whose union was seen as modeled on the cosmic hierogamy. But the important thing for the historian of religions is that the invention of agriculture enabled man to acquire a deeper insight into the cyclic nature of life. Of course the hunter knew that the animals he hunted gave birth in the spring, but it was the farmer who grasped the causal relationship between seed and harvest and the analogy between seed and semen. At the same time, the economic, social, and religious importance of woman became firmly established. So you see, it was by means of a technical discovery, that of agriculture, that a still more profound "mystery" than that confronting the hunter was revealed to man's consciousness: the discovery that the cosmos is a living organism, governed by a rhythm, by a cycle in which life is intimately and necessarily linked with death, since the seed cannot produce a rebirth except through its own death and burial. So this technical discovery revealed to man the mode of his own existence. It was the Neolithic era that first introduced those metaphors that persisted into Old Testament times and thus on to our own day: "Man is as the grass of the field," and so on—a theme we should not interpret as a lamentation over the ephemeral nature of vegetation but rather as a message of optimism: an understanding of the eternal cycle governing the vegetable kingdom and life in general. In short, to sum up my answer: it is beyond doubt that, as a result of a radical technological change, earlier religious values were, if not annihilated, at least diminished in importance, and it is clear, also, that the new values were founded on different economic conditions. But this new economy was to reveal a religious and creative meaning. The invention of agriculture was no less important for man's spiritual history than for the history of material civilization. The oneness of life and death was not clearly given in the hunter's experience of life; it became so once man began to cultivate the soil.

·R·   It seems to me that your thinking there is "Hegelian." In your account of these developments, it is as though the production of material facts, the changes in the material world, in the "infrastructures," had a meaning in that they led to a deepening of meaning. So that we have to regard events in the material world, historical events, as a series of conditions that permitted the revelation of a spiritual meaning. In fact, there is an entry in your *Journal*—for 2 March 1967—that says as much quite clearly: "The history of religions, as I personally understand it, is a 'saving discipline,' a 'liberating' discipline. Hermeneutics could become the only valid justification of history. A historical event will justify its occurrence *when it is understood.* That could mean that things happen, that history exists, solely in order to force men to understand them."

·E·   Yes, I believe that all these technical discoveries *created opportunities* for the human mind to grasp certain structures of being that were harder for it to grasp before they occurred. The hunter, needless to say, was aware of the rhythm of the seasons. But that rhythm was not the center of the theoretical construction that gave meaning to human life. Agriculture provided the opportunity for a vast synthesis. As soon as one discovers the cause of this new vision of the world—cultivation of the soil—one is spellbound. And by this "new vision" of the world I mean the identity, the homology, linking woman, earth, moon, fertility, vegetation; and again: night, fertility, death, initiation, resurrection. That whole system was made possible by agriculture. In the same way, think of that vast and splendid construction of the *imago mundi* that was later added to the representation of cyclic time, an image that did not become possible until the creation of cities. Of course man had always lived in oriented space, with a center and the four cardinal points: those are the data provided by his immediate experience of the world. But the city enriched that sense of space to the point where it presented itself as an image of the world. All urban cultures are based on the Neolithic heritage. And earlier values—the fertility of the earth, the importance of woman, the sacramental value of sexual union—all those values were integrated into the edifice of our urban culture. Today, that culture is in the process, not of vanishing altogether, but of

134

changing its structure. However, I don't believe that those primal revelations can vanish, because we shall continue to exist within the fundamental cosmic rhythm: day and night, winter and summer, everyday life and the life of dreams, light and darkness. We shall experience other, different religious forms, ones that will perhaps not be recognized as such and will themselves be conditioned in their turn by the language and society of the future. It is true that until now—and here I am not talking solely about "religion"—man has not yet been spiritually enriched by the latest technical discoveries in the way he was by the discovery of metalworking or alchemy.

Demystifying Demystification

·R·   You have now explained very clearly what you mean by a "hermeneutic attitude," and, at the same time, you have allowed us to glimpse the opposite attitude, one that aims at "demystification" and is common to Marx and the Marxists, Freud, and Lévi-Strauss and the structuralists. Presumably you owe something to all of those; but you stand on the opposite slope, as it were. Can you explain your position for us precisely?

·E·   It is certainly true that I have profited from all of the three currents of thought you have just mentioned. Just now I spoke of the radical importance of agriculture and therefore of a change in economic structures: Marx helped us to understand that. Freud, for his part, revealed the "embryology" of the mind; that's very important, but embryology is nevertheless no more than a brief instant in a being's acquisition of knowledge. And structuralism too has its uses. All the same, I believe that such a "demystifying" attitude is altogether too facile. All archaic or primitive men believe that their village is "the center of the world." To regard that belief as an illusion is easy, but it gets one absolutely nowhere. In doing so, one destroys the phenomenon by failing to observe it on its own level. The important thing, in fact, is to ask oneself *why* those men believe they live in the center of the world. If I try to understand a given tribe, it is

135

not in order to demystify its mythology, its theology, its customs, its representation of the world. I am trying to understand its culture and, in consequence, why those men believe what they do. And if I understand why they believe their village is the center of the world, then I am beginning to understand their mythology, their theology, and, consequently, their mode of existing in the world.

·R·   Besides, is it all that hard to understand? I remember a passage in which Merleau-Ponty, having talked about the primitive encampment, adds: "I arrive in a village for my vacation, elated at leaving my work and everyday companions behind me. I make myself at home in the village. It becomes the center of my life. . . . Our body and our perceptions perpetually urge us to accept the landscape they are presenting us with as the center of the world."

·E·   Yes, that experience, which we call sacred or religious, is an existential one. Because his body exists in space, any man orients himself by the four horizons and stands between above and below. He is naturally the center. Any culture is always built on existential experience.

·R·   When you talk about religions, about culture, even the most primitive and archaic, such as those of the aborigines, it is with infinite respect. For you, they are not just ethnological facts, they are works of creation. Religions, for you, are admirable human constructions, ripe with meaning and value. Just as much as the *Odyssey* or the *Divine Comedy* or Shakespeare.

·E·   I feel myself wholly contemporary with all the great political and social reforms or revolutions. All constitutions speak of equality among men: any human being whatsoever has exactly the same value as a genius in Paris or Boston or Moscow. That is a principle you scarcely ever find put into practice in the real world, alas. But when I make the acquaintance of an aborigine, then I can make it into a reality. I don't even approach him, as many anthropologists do, solely out of a curiosity to know more about institutions and economic phenomena. Knowledge of that sort is of the greatest

136

importance, undoubtedly, but stopping there is not the best method of grasping the contribution such men have made to the history of the human mind. What really interests me is finding out how a human being reacts when he is forced to exist in an Australian desert or in the Arctic. How did he manage, not merely to survive as a zoological species—as pigeons and seals have—but also to survive as a human being, to produce a culture, a religion, an aesthetic? They have lived there as human beings, which means to say that *they have created.* They have not remained content with behaving like seals or kangaroos. That is why I am so very proud of being a human being: not because I am a descendant of that prodigious Mediterranean culture but because I can recognize myself, as a human being, in the existence taken upon himself by an Australian aborigine. And that is why his culture interests me, and his religion, his mythology. That is the explanation of my sympathetic attitude; it is not some kind of infatuation with the past that makes me want to go back to the world of the Australian aborigines or the Eskimos. I want to *recognize* myself—in the philosophical sense—in my fellow man: as a Romanian, I was just like him, thousands of years ago. And that thought enables me to feel totally of my own time with him. If there really has been an original and important discovery made in our time, then it is certainly that: the unity of history and of the human mind and spirit. That is why I do not want, or try, to "demystify" things. One day we shall be blamed for our "demystification" by the descendants of those we once colonized. They will say to us: "You exalt the *creativity* of your Dante and your Vergil, but you *demystify* our mythologies and our religions. Your anthropologists never stop insisting on the socioeconomic presuppositions of our religion or our messianic and millenarist movements, thereby implying that our spiritual creations, *unlike yours,* never rise above material or political determining factors. In other words, *we primitives* are incapable of attaining the creative freedom of a Dante or a Vergil." Such a "demystifying" attitude ought to be arraigned in its turn, on charges of ethnocentrism, of Western "provincialism," and so, ultimately, be "demystified" itself.

137

·R· What you have just said also enables us to understand, once and for all, why the history of religions tends to be hermeneutic. If the religions and masterpieces of our culture are akin, then a hermeneutic stance is clearly unavoidable. Because, after all, it is obvious to everyone that linguistic analysis cannot exhaust our relationship with Rilke or Du Bellay. We all know that a poem cannot be reduced to its mechanics or to the historical conditions that made it possible. And if we do reduce it to those things, then so much the worse for us! If we understand that in the case of poetry, why can we no longer understand it in the case of a religion?

·E· I agree totally! That is why I always compare the world of the religious imagination with that of the poetic imagination. It makes it easier for someone unfamiliar with the domain of religions to enter it.

·R· Would you say that the domain of religion is a province of the imagination and symbolism?

·E· Yes, indeed. But it must also be said that in the beginning every imaginary universe was—to use an unfortunate term—a religious universe. I say "an unfortunate term," because in using it we are usually thinking solely in terms of Judeo-Christianity or pagan polytheism. The autonomy of dance, of poetry, of the plastic arts, is a recent invention. In the beginning, all those imaginary worlds possessed a religious value and function.

·R· But haven't they still, in a sense? On occasion, you yourself have spoken of "demystification in reverse," and you say that we must sometimes search in profane works of creation—in works of literature, say—for scenarios of initiation, for example.

·E· As you know, for a generation now, North American literary criticism, especially in the United States, has been looking in modern novels for themes of initiation, sacrifice, and mythical archetypes. I believe that the sacred is indeed camouflaged within the profane in the same way as the profane, for Freud and Marx, was camouflaged in the sa-

138

cred. I believe it is legitimate to recognize the patterns and rituals of initiation in certain novels. But all that is still a problem, and I very much hope that someone will go into it properly, really set about deciphering *the camouflage adopted by the sacred in a desacralized world.*

The Work of the Historian

Method: Going Back to the Beginning

·R· I shan't, of course, ask you to go back over the stages that the history of religions has passed through, even since the beginning of this century. You have already done that in your *The Quest: History and Meaning of Religion*. But I would like to know if there are any essential debts that you owe to your predecessors, your elders. I would like to hear you tell us about Georges Dumézil, who made you so welcome when you moved to Paris in 1945.

·E· I knew and admired Georges Dumézil's work long before I met him, which was in September 1945, a few days after my arrival in Paris. Since that time, my admiration for his genius has done nothing but grow, as he continues to develop and clarify his ideas about the Indo-European religions and mythologies. I doubt if there is another scholar in the whole world who can rival his prodigious linguistic erudition—he knows more than thirty languages and dialects!—or his vast knowledge of the history of religions, and who is at the same time endowed with such great literary talent. It was Georges Dumézil who injected new life into the study of Indo-European religions and myths. He demonstrated the importance of the tripartite conception of Indo-European society, that is to say its division into three superimposed layers corresponding to three functions: sovereignty, power, and fertility. Dumézil's example is all-important for the history of religions as an autonomous discipline, because he used his sociological and philosophical

141

knowledge to such brilliant effect in filling out his detailed philological and historical analysis of so many texts.

As far as my academic "career" goes in France, I owe that almost entirely to Georges Dumézil. It was he who invited me to give a course of lectures at the Ecole des Hautes Etudes—which I based on chapters from my *Patterns in Comparative Religion* and *The Myth of the Eternal Return*. And it was he again who sent Brice Parain the manuscript of my first book to be published by Gallimard.

·R· You have no difficulty in accepting Dumézil's structuralism but you reject that of Lévi-Strauss. Am I right?

·E· Yes, I accept structuralism as it is propounded by Dumézil, by Propp—and by Goethe. As you know, when Goethe was studying the morphology of plants, he came to the conclusion that it was possible to trace all vegetable forms back to what he called "the original plant," and he eventually identified that *Urpflanze* with the leaf. Propp was very struck by this notion, so much so that, in the Russian edition of his *Morphology of the Folktale,* every chapter is headed by a long quotation from Goethe's book. For my own part, in my early days at least, I thought that in order to keep sight of the forest among so many trees—facts, figures, and rituals—the historian of religions would do well to search for the "original plant" in his own field, for the primal image; in other words, for what happens when man confronts the sacred. In short, the kind of structuralism I consider fruitful consists in asking oneself about the essence of a set of phenomena, about the primordial order that is the basis of their meaning. I admire Lévi-Strauss very much as a writer, and I regard him as a remarkable mind; but, insofar as it excludes hermeneutics, there is nothing in his method that I can put to much use. A historian of religions, whatever his opinions—from Marxism to psychologism—thinks that his first duty, in practice, is to grasp the original *meaning* of a sacred phenomenon and then to interpret its history. So I don't quite see what a historian of religions is going to be able to do with structuralism in the Lévi-Straussian mold.

142

·R·   On your own path, what were the greatest obstacles? Your greatest uncertainties, your doubts?

·E·   One big difficulty was combining the writing of fiction with scholarly, scientific work. In my early days, in Romania, I was regarded by my superiors and my colleagues with a certain mistrust. They said to themselves: "A man who writes successful novels can't possibly be an objective thinker as well." It was only after the publication of my book on Yoga in French, and the favorable reviews it received from a number of great Indianists, that they were forced to accept that what I was doing was at least serious. As a result, I often postponed translation of my novels in later years, so as not to damage my credibility as a historian of religions and an Orientalist. It's true that now, paradoxically, it is a university press that is going to publish the English translation of *The Forbidden Forest* in the United States.

      Another difficulty was forcing myself to stick to a piece of scientific research when I was possessed by the subject for a novel or story. I went on giving my lectures, of course, but I wasn't really there.

·R·   So there were difficulties. But did you never experience any doubts about the validity of your propositions?

·E·   I never had any doubts, properly speaking, but I did suffer from a sort of perfectionism. To understand one section of my career, you have to realize that I come from a minor, provincial culture. I was afraid of not being as well informed as I ought to be. So I wrote to my masters, to my colleagues; and every summer I went abroad, to ransack the libraries. If I chanced on an interpretation different from my own, I was glad to find that it was possible to understand a given phenomenon from different viewpoints. Sometimes I altered a detail in my own work. But I never experienced any radical doubt that would have forced me to abandon my hypothesis or my method. What I wrote was based on my personal experience in India, the experience of those three years.

143

·R·   Your "method," you said just then. What is it?

·E·   The first point is to go to the best sources—the best translations, the best commentaries. To find out which those are, I question myself, my colleagues, and the specialists in the field. That way I am spared reading thousands of pages of little ultimate interest. My concern to know all the sources thoroughly was in fact one of the reasons why I devoted seven or eight years to Australian studies: I felt that it would be possible for me to read all the essential documents myself, something that would be impossible in the case of Africa or American Indian tribes.

      The second point, when one is approaching an archaic or traditional religion, is to begin at the beginning, in other words with the cosmogonic myth. How did the world come into being? Who created it? God, a demiurge, a mythic ancestor? Or was the world already there? Did a divine figure begin to transform it? Then come the myths concerning the origin of man and all his institutions.

·R·   Would you say, to paraphrase a well-known epigram about phantasms, that the myth of the origin is the origin of myths?

·E·   All myths are variants of the myth of the origin, because the creation of the world is the model for all creation. The origin of the world is the model for that of man, plants, and even sexuality and death and, again, institutions. All mythology has a beginning and an end: in the beginning, the cosmogony; at the end, eschatology—a return of the mythic ancestors or the coming of the messiah. So the historian of religions will not see mythology as an incoherent agglomeration of myths but as a single corpus endowed with meaning—in short, as a "sacred history."

·R·   The question to which the myth of the origin is an answer is, in another form, the question put by Leibniz, which, as we know, occupies such an important place in the work of Heidegger: "Why is there something rather than nothing?"

·E·   Yes, it is the same question. Why does the real—in other words, the universe—exist? How did the real come to be realized? That is why I have often referred, in connection with the myths of primitive man, to an "archaic ontology." For primitive man, as for the man of traditional societies, objects in the external world have no autonomous intrinsic value. A thing or an action acquires a *value* and thereby becomes real because it has now become part, in one way or another, of a reality that transcends it. So that one could say, as I suggested in *The Myth of the Eternal Return,* that archaic ontology has a Platonic structure.

The Unexplained

·R· So the difficulty of acquiring information explains a certain lack of African material in your work?

·E· Fifteen years or so ago I started on a projected history of primitive religions. I published only the one short book on Australian aboriginal religions. The vastness of the documented material available made me hesitate when confronted with Africa. Starting with Griaule and his pupils, African studies in France have renewed our understanding of African religions to such an extent. . . .

·R· Did you know Marcel Griaule?

·E· Yes, quite well, and I felt that his discoveries and interpretations confirmed the direction my own work was taking. With Griaule, with his *Conversations with Ogotemmeli,* we finally said goodbye to the idiotic image people used to have of "savages." It was also the end of the "prelogical mentality," a theme that Lévy-Bruhl himself had in any case abandoned. When it was seen that Griaule succeeded in acquiring his knowledge of the extraordinary and rigorous theology of the Dogons only after he had spent long periods living among them, it became clear that ordinary travelers must always lack such knowledge. On the basis of what we now know about the Dogons, one is justified in supposing the existence of a solidly constructed and similarly subtle theology among other such peoples and in any "archaic" thought. That is why Griaule's work is of such great importance, not only for ethnologists but also for historians of

145

religions, who up till then had been far too inclined merely
to regurgitate Frazer.

·R·   I was told a story about Griaule. After his death, a
number of his friends, Dogons and Europeans, met one day
to celebrate his memory. During the meal they saw Griaule
among them. When you hear such stories, do you accept
them as accounts of possible events?

·E·   These things are possible when the people to
whom they happen belong to a certain spiritual universe. If
the Dogons saw Griaule after his death, that is certainly a sign
that he was spiritually one of them.

·R·   So in this area of phenomena not covered by
everyday reasoning and science—apparitions after death, for
example—there are things that are possible or impossible according to our spiritual quality?

·E·   That is what an Italian ethnologist and historian of
religions, Ernesto De Martino, asserted in his book *Il mondo
magico,* which contains studies of a number of parapsychological or "spirit" phenomena among "primitive" peoples.
Martino recognized the reality of these phenomena in primitive cultures but not in ours. He believed in the authenticity
of the apparitions brought about by a shaman, but he denied
it to the analogous apparitions produced during our spiri-
tualist séances. This was because, for him, nature itself is
culturalmente condizionata. Certain "natural" laws vary according to the idea of "nature" that different cultures have
acquired. With us, nature obeys the law of gravity, for example; but that law is not a law among archaic societies: hence
the possibility of parapsychological phenomena. It is a very
controversial theory, needless to say, but I find it interesting.
Personally, I am unable to make any pronouncement where
parapsychology is concerned. However, it is permissible to
hope that we shall know more about the subject a generation
hence.

·R·   I have heard it said that a certain Marxist geographer of great repute, and an African specialist as well, as-

serts in private that the local African gods are real forces.

·E· "Real forces," yes, we know that. But to believe in the coherent and, as it were, "incarnate" manifestation of those forces, that is something else again. When, for example, an aborigine talks about certain cosmic or even psychosomatic forces embodied in a superhuman being, it is extremely difficult to be sure that the notion we are forming of such things is the same as the one the aborigines themselves have. At all events, what you told me just now about the Marxist geographer is very interesting. That proves he is a genuinely scientific thinker: he accepts that facts are facts.

·R· And how is one not to be disturbed by the fact that thinkers like Nietzsche and Heidegger speak of "gods," think in terms of "gods"? Unless we are to believe that they intended no more than a poetic metaphor....

·E· Nietzsche, Heidegger, and Walter Otto, too, the great German specialist in Greek mythology and religion, who in his book on the Homeric gods likewise asserted those gods' reality. But what exactly did these scholars and philosophers mean by this "reality" of the gods? Did they think of the reality of the gods in the same way as an ancient Greek did? What is very disturbing, in fact, is that we are not dealing here with childish or superstitious comments but with assertions that spring from mature and profound thought processes.

·R· While we are on the subject of stories that leave one wondering, yesterday I reread a short passage in your *Journal* describing an account a woman friend of yours gave of how once, in place of a barn wall, she saw a garden glowing with light. Just once, and never a hint of it again. You tell the story and just leave it at that.

·E· Yes, why add any comment? There are certain transhuman experiences that we are forced to accept as facts. But what means do we have of knowing their nature?

·R· But similar things have happened to you?

·E· I hesitate to answer that.

revealed religions—Judaism, Christianity, Islam—are "traditional." In practice, they all regard themselves as guardians of a *traditio,* a "sacred history" that not only constitutes a total explanation of the world and a justification of humanity's present condition but also presents itself as a *summum* of exemplary models for all human behavior and activities. All these models are reputed to be of transhuman origin or divine inspiration. But, in the great majority of traditional societies, certain teachings are esoteric and, as such, are transmitted by means of an initiation. Now, today, the term "Tradition" is very often used to mean "esotericism," an unbroken chain of arcane knowledge. As a result, anyone who asserts that he is a follower of the "Tradition" is letting it be understood that he is an "initiate," that he is the depository of "a secret teaching." And that, even in the best of cases, is an illusion.

·R· One of the meanings of the history of religions, for you, is to salvage what deserves salvaging, to preserve values held to be essential. However, although the historian of religions must strive to understand everything, he cannot justify everything. He cannot wish to perpetuate or restore all beliefs, all rituals. Like each one of us, he must be selective about all those values and insert them into an order. How do you reconcile your respect for everything that is human with that inevitable moral choice? For example, certain humanitarian movements have recently protested to UNESCO against the practice of clitoral excision. If UNESCO were to consult you on this subject, what would your answer be?

·E· I should advise UNESCO without hesitation to condemn such excision. As a rite it is not of any great importance. There is nothing primitive about it; in fact, it was introduced only quite recently. It is in no way central to the religious concepts or initiations of the peoples who practice it, and it has no fundamental value for their religious or moral behavior. In short, it is merely the result of a growth that I myself would call "cancerous": at once dangerous and monstrous. The abandonment of such a custom is totally desirable.

150

·R·   The third volume of your *History of Religious Ideas* will cover the period that stretches from the birth of Islam to the "atheist theologies" of our own time. So that, for you, atheism constitutes part of the history of religions. We know from your *Journal,* moreover, that you met Tillich and certain "theologians of the death of God" in the United States. Is this theme of "the death of God" the limiting concept of the history of religions?

·E·   I must begin by pointing out that the theme of "the death of God" is not a radical innovation. In short, it is a revival of the notion of the *deus otiosus,* the idle god—the god who made the world, then left it to shift for itself; and that is a notion found in a number of archaic religions. However, it is true that the theology of "the death of God" is extremely important, because it is the sole religious creation of the modern Western world. What it presents us with is the final step in the process of desacralization. For the historian of religions its interest is considerable, since this ultimate phase shows the "sacred" reaching a perfect state of camouflage or, more accurately, becoming wholly identified with the "profane."

      It is no doubt still too early to grasp the meaning of this "desacralization" and of the theologies of "the death of God" contemporary with it; too soon to predict its future. But the questions it poses are these: to what degree can the "profane" become "sacred," and to what degree is a radically secularized existence, without God or gods, capable of constituting the point of departure for a new type of "religion"? I think I can make out three broad types of answer to that question. First, that of the "theologians of the death of God": beyond the destruction of all the symbols, rituals, and concepts of the Christian churches, they still hope—thanks to a paradoxical and mysterious *coincidentia oppositorum*—that this new awareness of the radically profane nature of the world and human existence can be used as the foundation for a new mode of religious experience, so that for them the death of "religion" is not the death of "faith" but in fact its very opposite. Another answer consists in regarding the historical forms of the *sacred/profane* opposition as secondary, so that

151

the disappearance of religions would in no way imply the disappearance of religiosity, and the constant transformation of sacred values into profane values would count less than the permanent meeting that man has with himself, less than the experience of his own condition. Last, the third answer: one can think that the opposition between sacred and profane has no meaning except for *religions* and that *Christianity is not a religion.* In other words, the Christian no longer has to live, as archaic man did, in a cosmos, but in history. But what is "history"? And what is the value of this temptation, or this attempt, to sacralize it? What world is it expected to save?

๛ Imaginary Figures

Religion and the Sacred

·R·   You must certainly remember the opening of
Lévi-Strauss's *Totemism:* "It is with totemism as with hysteria.
No sooner did we take it into our heads to doubt that it was
possible to isolate certain phenomena in an arbitrary way, and
to group them together so as to use them as the diagnostic
signs of a disease or of an objective institution, than those
symptoms themselves disappeared, or proved intractable to
unifying interpretations." Is it not the same with religion as
with totemism or hysteria? Or, to put it another way, if the
history, or the science, of religions has an object, what is it?

·E·   That object is the *sacred.* But how do we set limits
to the sacred? It's very difficult. What seems to me totally
impossible, at all events, is to imagine how the human mind
could function without the conviction that there is something
irreducibly *real* in the world. It is impossible to imagine how
consciousness could appear without conferring a *meaning* on
man's impulses and experiences. Consciousness of a real and
meaningful world is intimately linked with the discovery of
the sacred. Through experience of the sacred the mind
grasped the difference between what is revealed as real, po-
tent, rich, and meaningful and that which is deficient in those
qualities—in other words, the chaotic and perilous flux of
things, their fortuitous and meaningless appearances and dis-
appearances. But here I must stress this point yet again: the
sacred is not a stage in the history of consciousness, it is a

structural element *of* that consciousness. In the most archaic phases of culture, *to live as a human being* was in itself *a religious act,* since eating, sexual activity, and labor all had a sacramental value. Experience of the sacred is inherent in man's mode of being in the world. Without experience of the real—and of what is not real—the human being would be unable to construct himself. And it is on the basis of that fact that the historian of religions begins to study the different religious forms.

·R· So the sacred is the keystone of religious experience. But it is different from a physical phenomenon or from a historical fact, for example, in that it cannot be revealed except by means of a "phenomenology." Am I right?

·E· Quite right. And to begin with, when we think of the sacred we must not limit it to divine figures. The sacred does not necessarily imply belief in God or gods or spirits. I repeat, it is the experience of a reality and the source of an awareness of existing in the world. What is this consciousness that makes us men? It is the result of that experience of the sacred, of the division that occurs between the real and the unreal. If experience of the sacred lies essentially within the province of consciousness, then it is clear that the sacred cannot be recognized "from outside." It is by means of internal experience that each individual will be able to recognize it in the religious acts of a Christian or a "primitive" man.

·R· The sacred stands in opposition to the profane and is itself ambivalent, not only because its two poles are life and death but also because it simultaneously attracts and repels. Those are the broad themes of both your *The Sacred and the Profane* and your *Patterns in Comparative Religion,* in which you quote the conclusions—similar to your own—reached by Roger Caillois in his *L'Homme et le sacré.* All that is well known. But, in an introduction you wrote in 1964 for your essay *The Sacred and the Profane,* you say: "There remains a problem to which I have so far referred only indirectly: How far can the 'profane' itself become 'sacred'? How far is a radically secularized existence, without God or gods, capable of constituting the starting point of a new type of 'religion'?" Let us take a simple example: Is Lenin's tomb "sacred"?

·E·   For the historian of religions the problem is, as you suggest, to recognize the survival of the sacred, of its expressions, its structures, however well camouflaged or distorted, in a world that presents itself, consciously and resolutely, as profane. From this point of view it is possible to recognize several great biblical myths in Marx and Marxism: the redemptive role of the Just Man, the ultimate eschatological struggle between Good (proletariat) and Evil (bourgeoisie), followed by the inauguration of the Golden Age. However, I am not going to say that Lenin's tomb is religious in essence, even though, while being a revolutionary symbol, it does perform the function of a religious symbol.

·R·   But what about the divinization of Roman emperors? Are we dealing there with the profane and laical survival of a sacred form or with a true archaic form of the sacred?

·E·   With the truly sacred, both archaic and modern. The apotheosis of the Roman emperor derives directly from the royal ideology of the East. It is the sovereign, the chief, the Imperator, who is responsible for order and fertility within his empire. He is the guarantor of the cosmic cycles, the order of the seasons, and success—*fortuna.* He embodies the genius that protects the empire, as the kings of Mesopotamia and the divine pharaohs did in earlier times.

·R·   I seem to remember that Malraux, in his *Anti-Memoirs,* recalls asking Mao Tse-tung whether he knew that he was "the last emperor." And the "bronze emperor" agreed. You see the Roman emperor as a sacred human being in the way that ancient emperors of China were: as embodying a link between earth and heaven, responsible for maintaining order in the world. Lenin you see as no more than a survival of the sacred. What about Mao Tse-tung?

·E·   Mao certainly had the right to call himself "the last emperor." He was the guardian and interpreter of the right doctrine and, in everyday life, the person responsible for his people's peace and well-being. He was indeed an emperor, almost mythologically and archetypically so. He was an extension of the Chinese imperial tradition. Only the vocabulary had changed; the function remained the same.

·R·   What criterion entitles us to differentiate between the last emperor, Mao, and the last tsar, Lenin? It seems to me that you are implicitly distinguishing between a "true sacred," which verges on the transcendent, and a "false sacred."

·E·   It is certainly true that the relation with transcendence is lacking in modern political ideologies. But two things still remain of the feeling for the sacred: the leader's fundamental responsibility, and a messianic hope. I don't know how Stalin saw himself. But read the poets: he was seen as a sun, as the unique Man. Those are not "transcendental" images, of course, but they are, at the very least, "transhuman," superhuman. The myth of Stalin reveals a nostalgia for the archetype. There is no "degradation" that does not reflect a lost, or confusedly desired, higher state.

Myth, Ritual, Initiation

·R·   So the sacred is the essence of whatever is religious. But there is presumably no religion without rites, without myths, without symbols, and perhaps, to begin with, without initiation: that ritual by means of which the being is born to the myths and symbols of religious community. Rituals, myths, symbols—how are these things linked?

·E·   You have just summarized the history of religions, and it would take whole books to answer your question! The myth tells a sacred story. That is to say, it recounts a primordial event that took place in the beginning of time and involved characters who are either gods or heroes and whose deeds created civilization. That is why the myth is the foundation of absolute truth. That is why, since it reveals how a reality came to be as it is, myth constitutes the exemplary model not only of rituals but also of all meaningful human activity: provision of food, sexuality, labor, education. That being so, man in his everyday activities is imitating the gods, repeating their actions. I have often given the example of a certain tribe in New Guinea: among them, a single myth serves as the model for all activities relating to navigation, from the construction of the boat (and the sexual taboos that that entails) to the gestures used in fishing and even the courses the boats must follow. The fisherman, when he makes a particular ritual gesture, is not imploring the god's help; he is imitating that god, identifying with him. Again, what we must see, what we must understand, is the *existential* value of the myth. Myths still man's anguish, make him feel secure. That Polynesian, when he ventures out onto the ocean, does so without fear because he is sure that, as long as he exactly repeats the gestures of the Ancestor, or the god, then his ultimate success is already *there* in the order of things. This confidence is one of the forces that have enabled man to survive, in a real way.

·R· Yes, just as "the symbol gives one to think," so the ritual helps one to live, and myth is sometimes the underpinning of our destiny. I remember an entry in your *Journal* where you say that you would like to clarify the way in which the history of religions can help to reveal the transcendent in everyday life. Moreover, your *Journal* often reveals you living out a mythic situation yourself: you are the man exiled from his homeland, the man who is searching for his path. But you are not just that lost man born in March 1907; you are Ulysses, and that image, that thought, sustains you.

On another level, you have sometimes compared Platonic ontology and archaic ontology. Do you see a kinship between the Idea and the "mythic model"?

·E· Both things certainly involve anamnesis. According to Plato, knowledge consists in the soul's remembering Ideas that it had gazed on in Heaven. Among the aborigines, the neophyte is brought into the presence of a stone object, the *tjurunga,* which represents his mythical ancestor. Not only is he taught the tribe's sacred history, told of the deeds by which the Ancestor founded civilization; it is also revealed to him that he himself *is* that Ancestor. It is exactly the same as the Platonic anamnesis!

157

·R·   Initiation is usually thought of as a means of access to the sacred. Can it not also be a demystification, on the lines of: "When you were a child, you believed. But now you must know"?

·E·   Yes, that type of initiation is found mainly at the elementary levels of culture. It was undoubtedly the most ancient form of southeastern Australian puberty rites. The boy child, having been taken away from his mother—in other words, from nature—is terrorized by the bull-roarers, then circumcised. After that, he is shown how the terrifying voice of the spirits is produced, and he is invited to make them speak himself. So there is an element of demystification involved, but there is also a transition to a higher plane of intelligence. The initiate isn't told that the supernatural being doesn't exist; he is simply shown that one of its so-called manifestations ought not to frighten anyone but the uninitiated. The initiate, once freed from his childish belief, is invited to discover his identity with the *tjurunga,* the petrified body of the Ancestor, who, having accomplished everything he had to do on earth, has withdrawn to heaven. For completeness' sake I should add that there is a further initiation ceremony reserved solely for witch doctors, for shamans.

·R·   You have pondered a great deal over the collapse of traditional initiation and over what replaces it in our own society. I shall simply put this question to you: How are we to tell children that they are sexual and mortal beings?

·E·   Today, not only has sexuality been desacralized, demystified, but death has too: it is ignored. The sight and thought of it are repressed. In a profane society it is very difficult to initiate children into these two great mysteries. I have no answer. Is it actually possible for a child to understand death or sexuality? I don't know what one ought to say.

·R·   It is presumably nostalgia for "traditional" initiation that explains, in part at least, the success of Castaneda's books. What status would you accord them?

·E·   Some anthropologists accept his evidence, others

deny it any authenticity whatever. In fact his dissertation, *The Teachings of Don Juan, a Yaqui Way of Knowledge,* was accepted by the University of California. He sent me the proofs for my advice, because of my work on shamanism. I had just finished teaching a course at the University of Santa Barbara, and I had stopped over for a few days in Los Angeles. Unfortunately, I didn't have the time to read his dissertation there and then. I read the book later, when Castaneda was already famous. What interested me most was his description of the meeting where they "smoke." He makes it clear that the important thing is not just smoking such and such a drug but doing so in a consecrated, oriented, specific place, in the master's presence, and in a certain frame of mind. In a certain position, the smoker will have a vision; in another, he won't. So Castaneda established the importance of the ritual—of the ritual, even philosophical, context—of drugs. That was something that needed to be said to all those young people who think that smoke alone can waft them to beatitude.

Sacred Men

·R·   You have devoted particular attention to the yogin, the shaman, and the alchemist. What do you see those three as having in common?

·E·   Whether it is a matter of ordinary or extraordinary initiation, the scenario is always that of a symbolic death followed by a rebirth, a resurrection. Take the yogin: he dies to the profane world, leaves his family, and changes his name and sometimes his language. In my book on Yoga I indicated how abundant the terms denoting death and rebirth are in the vocabulary of the yogins. But the same theme is also to be found in the teachings of the Buddha, even though he had broken with tradition on so many points. Socrates talks of a "maieutics." Philo, too, makes abundant use of the metaphor of childbirth to denote accession to the life of the spirit. And Saint Paul speaks of procreation through faith.

·R·   In your *The Forge and the Crucible* you say that the alchemist projects this initiatory death onto matter.

159

·E· The initiatory element in alchemy is the torture and putting-to-death of metals in order to "perfect" them, to transform them into gold. The acquisition of the philosopher's stone, and of gold, coincides with that of the alchemist's new personality.

·R· So alchemy stands halfway between archaic initiation and philosophical initiation?

·E· In a way, yes. But this initiatory element in alchemy is not what constitutes alchemy. Alchemy, for me, is the last stage in the work that began with the discovery of metallurgy. The "founder" transforms mineral into metal, and the alchemist takes over the work of nature and time in order to acquire the philosopher's stone and gold—the equivalent of immortality.

·R· You have not paid the same degree of attention to the priest, or even to the prophet, as to the yogin, the shaman, and the alchemist.

·E· So much work, and such good work, had already been done on the priest and the priesthood that I preferred to turn my attention to areas that were less well known or were even dismissed with contempt: the shaman, for example, who was regarded as mentally ill or a mere magician. Apart from which, it seemed to me that if I was to understand the prophets and prophecy, then I had to begin with shamanism.

·R· But aren't you perhaps more drawn to the "esoteric" than to the "exoteric," to the mystic rather than to institutions, to the archaic rather than the modern?

·E· No doubt I am. I have taken an interest in what is termed the esoteric side of certain things—the initiatory rituals of shamanism, of Tantrism, and of "primitive" societies generally—because there was something there that was hard to grasp and that one scarcely ever came across in books. As far as the archaic is concerned, I could see that the world's "traditional" or "primitive" societies were in the process of vanishing, that in another human lifetime they

160

would be gone, and that the ethnologists and anthropologists studying them were scarcely concerning themselves at all with grasping the coherence, the nobility, and the beauty of such societies' mythological systems and theologies.

·R·   But behind those reasons, behind the professor of the history of religions and the author of all those scholarly books, I wonder if there isn't a kind of Romanian Rimbaud lurking: "The Whites disembark.... The cannon.... One must submit to baptism, to wearing clothes.... The pagan blood returns." I have found no resentment in you, anywhere. But no feeling of rebellion? Not ever? I wonder whether behind your love for untamed peoples there isn't a fund of anger, an anger you have never expressed, against the powerful and the hyperrational, all those pontificators, bankers, and strategists, all those mercenaries and do-gooders spawned by a machine-age intelligence. I try to imagine you twenty years old still, in Bucharest. At the root of that reasoned, reasonable interest in the shaman, in the world's witch doctors as a whole, and in all those men who live by poverty and vision, I glimpse a Romanian brother of Rimbaud.

·E·   In the very depths of my being, perhaps there is that feeling of rebellion against certain aggressive forms of possession, of power, the powers of subjugation acquired by a mechanical civilization. But above all I sensed among the inspired and ecstatic mystics I have studied the presence of the primal sources of religion and art and metaphysics. I have always felt that to understand one of those unknown, or despised, dimensions of the history of the human spirit was not merely to enrich our knowledge but to contribute to the regeneration and development of the human spirit's creativity, in our world and in our time.

Dreams and Religion

·R·   What links are there between dreams and religion?

·E·   Dreams undoubtedly possess mythological structures, but they are experienced in isolation, so that the

161

whole man is never present in them. The religious experience is a daytime one, and man's relationship with the sacred engages his being in its totality. The resemblances between dreams and myth are obvious, but the difference between them is an essential one: there is the same gulf between the two as between an act of adultery and *Madame Bovary;* that is, between a simple experience and a creation of the human spirit.

·R· Isn't the dream the basic material of the religious? The dream, in which the dead live again, in which chimeras are real, in which another world appears? And is the difference between sleep and waking unconnected with the difference between the sacred and the profane?

·E· For me, the sacred is always the revelation of the real, an encounter with that which saves us by giving meaning to our existence. If that encounter and that revelation take place in a dream, then we are not conscious of it. As for knowing whether the dream is at the origin of religion . . . . It has in fact been said that animism was the first form of religion and that the dream experience nourished such beliefs. But people don't say that nowadays. And I believe, personally, that it is through consideration of the sky's immensity that man is led to a revelation of transcendence, of the sacred.

·R· The birth of the divine occurred, not in sleeping man, but in man wide-eyed and wide awake?

·E· Sleeping man contributes a great deal; but I believe that the fundamental experience is that of man awake.

·R· Obviously, when I ask you questions about dreams and myth, I have Jung in mind. And I should like to know how much you owe to each other as far as your work was concerned.

·E· I have a great admiration for Jung, both for the thinker and for the kind of man he was. I met him in August 1950, at the Eranos Conference in Ascona. After half an hour's conversation I felt I was listening to a Chinese Sage

162

or an east European peasant, still rooted in the Earth Mother yet close to Heaven at the same time. I was enthralled by the wonderful simplicity of his *presence,* by the spontaneity, the erudition, and the humor of his conversation. He was seventy-five at that time. After that I saw him again almost every year, either in Ascona or Zurich; the last time, a year before his death, was in 1960. And at each meeting I was deeply impressed by the fullness, and what I must call the "wisdom," of his life.

His work, that's hard for me to judge. I haven't read it all, and I have no experience of psychoanalysis, either Freudian or Jungian. Jung took an interest in both Yoga and shamanism. And an interest in alchemy was another area of common ground between us. As you know, I was still a high-school student when I became interested in alchemy, and I'm fairly sure I wrote my first book on Indian alchemy before Jung himself had published anything in that field. But by the time I met him, he'd written *Psychology and Alchemy.* In other words, our paths ran parallel. For Jung, alchemy is an image, or model, for his "individuation." For me, it is what I explained just now, with reference to *The Forge and the Crucible.*

I don't know exactly what I owe to Jung. I have read a good many of his books, notably *The Psychology of Transference.* I had long conversations with him at Eranos. He believed in a kind of fundamental unity of the collective unconscious, and I likewise consider that there is a fundamental unity underlying all religious experience.

·R· Rereading your *Journal,* I had the feeling that the essential place Jung accorded the image of the "center" was something he owed to you.

·E· That's possible. I gave a lecture on that theme at Eranos in 1950. But it may have been through one of his disciples, Neumann, that Jung came to perceive the possible advantage to be derived from the "center" in psychoanalytic therapy.

·R· You have both written a great deal about archetypes.

163

·E·   But not in the same sense. I was wrong to subtitle my *Myth of the Eternal Return* "Archetypes and Repetition." There was such a danger of confusion with Jung's terminology. For him, archetypes are structures of the collective unconscious. I was using the term with reference to Plato and Saint Augustine. I gave it the sense of "exemplary model," revealed in myth and reactualized through ritual. I should have said "Paradigms and Repetition."

Myth and Writing

Myth, Literature, Wisdom

·R·   At Queneau's request you wrote a chapter on oral literature for the *Encyclopédie de la Pléiade*. It was a good idea to ask a historian of myth and folklore to cover that area. And you approached oral literature in the same spirit as you did the world of myth. The entry in your *Journal* for 21 August 1964 includes this passage: "Every time I try to talk about oral literature I must begin by reminding myself that these creations are reflections, not of external realities— geography, customs, institutions, and so on—or of historical events, but of the dramas, the tensions, and the hopes of man, his value and meanings, in a word, concrete spiritual *life* as it achieves fruition in culture."

·E·   I certainly think that anyone who wants to under-stand oral literature must first rediscover the world of significations from which it springs.

·R·   Myth and literature: you don't link those two terms solely from the historical point of view. With your work as a historian of religions in mind, you wrote on 15 December 1960: "Ultimately, what I have been doing for more than fifteen years is not totally foreign to *literature*. It may be that my research will be regarded one day as an at-tempt to rediscover the forgotten sources of literary in-spiration."

·E·   It is well known that literature, oral or written, is

165

the offspring of mythology and that it inherits its parent's functions: narrating adventures, narrating the *significant* things that have happened in the world. But why is it so important to know what is happening, to know what happens to the marquise when she takes tea at five o'clock? I believe that all narration, even that of a very ordinary event, is an extension of the stories told by the great myths that explain how this world came into being and how our condition has come to be as we know it today. I think that an interest in narration is part of our mode of being in the world. It answers our essential need to hear what has happened, what men have done, what they have the power to do: risks, adventures, trials of all sorts. We are not here in the world like stones, unable to move, or like flowers or insects, whose life is wholly laid out in advance: we are beings of *adventure.* And man will never be able to do without listening to stories.

·R· 　　　In the past, you have linked the myths of aborigines with Joyce's *Ulysses.* On 7 March 1963, you wrote: "We are wonderstruck, we marvel, just like the aborigines, when Leopold Bloom stops off in a bar and orders a beer." Doesn't that mean that in order to attain self-consciousness man needs a mirror, a record—words? In short, that the world becomes real only through an imaginative process?

·E· 　　　Yes. One becomes oneself when one learns one's history.

·R· 　　　Literature inherits the functions of the myth. Can we say that myth dies, and literature is born, with the invention of writing?

·E· 　　　First, let me point out that, before the birth of literature, there appeared the religions of the Book. But to answer your question: perhaps what disappears with writing is only the visibly evident universe of the myth. Think of the medieval romances—for example, the Grail quest. There can be no doubt that myth continues to exist within writing. Writing does not destroy mythic creativity.

166

·R· You were talking just now about the importance
of storytelling, and in your *Journal* you are extremely critical of some modern literature and art. You assign philosophical nihilism, political or moral anarchism, and meaningless art to one and the same category.

·E· Meaninglessness seems to me the most antihuman
thing there is. To be human is to seek for meaning, for
value—to invent it, project it, reinvent it. So the triumph of
the meaningless, in certain areas of modern art, seems to
me a revolt against humanity. It is a desiccation, a sterili-
zation—and a great bore! I accept sterility, boredom, mo-
notony, but only as a spiritual exercise: the preparation
for mystic contemplation. In that case, there is a meaning
there. But to offer the meaningless as an object for "contemplation" and aesthetic delight, that I don't accept, I rebel
against it utterly. Naturally I see that it is sometimes a cry
of distress uttered by certain artists in protest against the
meaninglessness of modern existence. But repeating that
message ad infinitum and thereby merely compounding the
meaninglessness—that I don't see the point of.

·R· You likewise reject ugliness in art. I am thinking
of what you have to say about Francis Bacon, for example.

·E· I understand perfectly his reason for searching
out ugliness as the object of his plastic creation. But at the
same time I have resistance to that ugliness, because we can
already see it everywhere around us—today more than ever
before. Why add more ugliness to the universal ugliness
into which we are being plunged deeper and deeper every
day?

·R· By turning away from storytelling, literature has
sometimes failed, in your eyes, to satisfy one of man's
essential needs. Do you think that the cinema, on the contrary, has proved to be one of the areas in which modern
man has favored the myth?

·E· Yes, I do think that the cinema still possesses that
vast possibility of recounting a myth, and of camouflaging it
in the most marvelous way, not only in the profane but even

167

within things that are almost degraded or degrading. The art of the cinema can use symbols so skillfully that you don't even see them any more; but you sense them, afterwards.

·R· What films, what film-makers, are you thinking of in particular?

·E· I've been to the cinema so little in the past few years that I can't answer that question as I would like. But let us say Fellini's *Clowns*. When I see a film like that, I am very aware of the vast potential the cinema has for recreating the great mythic themes and for making use of certain major symbols in unusual forms.

·R· It's not hard to guess what books you wouldn't take to a desert island. But which would you take?

·E· Some of Balzac's novels, some of Dostoevski's . . . The second part of *Faust* and Goethe's autobiography . . . Milarepa's biography, and his poems: they are more than just poetry, they are magic, spellbinding. Shakespeare, without doubt. Novalis and some of the other German Romantics. And Dante, above all. I'm just giving you names off the top of my head; there would be others, of course.

·R· You haven't mentioned the Bible. Do you read it simply as a historian of religions?

·E· I love Ecclesiastes. And, like everyone, I have my favorite psalms. I like the whole of the New Testament. Our contemporaries tend to prefer the Gospel according to Saint John, but I like all four, and some of the Epistles. Revelations I find interesting as a document, but it's not one of my favorite books. After all, I know a lot of other apocalypses—Iranian, Jewish, Greek. Needless to say, there are several ways of reading the Bible. That of the Christian, the believer, or rather that of the man reminding himself that he ought to be a believer, a Christian: one forgets that every day. There is the historian's way. And another too: one can read it as a very great and very beautiful model of how to write.

168

·R· One entry in your *Journal* shows you reading and rereading the *Bhagavad Gītā*.

·E· Yes, it is one of the great books that formed me. I always find a new, deep meaning in it. It is a very consoling book because, as you know, Krishna reveals to Arjuna all the possibilities for salvation—in other words, of finding a meaning for one's existence. And I think it is the keystone of Hinduism, the synthesis of the Indian spirit and all its paths, all its philosophies, all its techniques for attaining salvation. The great problem was this: in order to "save oneself" in the Indian sense—to free oneself from this world of evil—must one abandon life and society, retire into the forest like the rishis of the Upanishads, like the yogins? Must one dedicate oneself exclusively to mystic devotion? Well, Krishna reveals that everyone, starting from any profession whatever, can succeed in reaching him, in finding the meaning of existence, in saving himself from this void of illusions and ordeals. All vocations can lead to salvation. It is not only the mystics, the philosophers, or yogins who will experience deliverance, but also the man of action, the man who stays in the world, on condition that his actions there are in conformity with the model that Krishna reveals. I said that it is a consoling book; but it is at the same time the justification of human existence in history. It is constantly said that the Indian spirit disengages itself from history, and that is true; but not in the *Bhagavad Gītā*. Arjuna was armed in readiness, the great battle was about to be joined, and Arjuna had doubts, because he knew that he was going to kill and thereby commit a mortal sin. And Krishna then reveals to him that everything can be different if he does not pursue a personal goal, if he does not kill out of hate, out of a desire for gain, or in order to feel himself a hero. Everything can be different if he accepts the combat as an impersonal thing, as something that is done in the name of god, in the name of Krishna, and—in the words of that extraordinary formula—if he "renounces the fruit of his actions." In war, to "renounce the fruit of one's actions" is to renounce the fruit of the *sacrifice* you are making—by killing

169

or being killed—in the same way as you would make an offering, almost a ritual offering, to god. In that way one can be saved from the infernal cycle of karma: our actions cease to be the seed of further actions. You know the doctrine of karma, of course, the doctrine of universal causality: everything one does will have an effect later on; every deed lays the foundation for another deed. Well, if, in the midst of one's activity, even warlike activity, one doesn't think of oneself but abandons "the fruit of one's action," then that infernal cycle of cause and effect is abolished.

·R·   "Renouncing the fruit of one's action"—is that a rule you have adopted yourself?

·E·   I think so, yes, because I was taught, and I became accustomed, to behave in that way, which I find very human and very enriching. I believe that we must do things, that we must follow our vocations, but without thinking of reward.

·R·   Rereading your *Journal,* I was touched by a passage where you talk about a cat that woke you up by yowling in a particularly hideous way; and you say that the way consists in . . .

·E·   In *loving.* Yes, there's no doubt about that. And it is what Christ said. It is possibly the fundamental rule of all the forms of ascesis in the world; but it is above all the way indicated by Christ. It is the only form of behavior that really enables one to cope with evil—well, of course, my poor cat wasn't exactly evil incarnate! But let's say: to respond with love to something that exasperates or terrifies you. And that can be proved.

·R·   You say that suddenly you began to imagine the loathsome cat as a wretched cat, and then—though it wasn't the first time it had happened to you—you felt yourself totally changed. And that was what you had learned from the teachings of your spiritual masters.

·E·   Exactly. And then I was glad that a cat had reminded me of that great lesson, which I had learned from those "spiritual masters" and from Jesus, from Christ. A cat, too, had forced me to understand that lesson.

·R· When I see men much more spiritually advanced than myself, it is something that always leaves me with a question in my mind. I ask myself: is it through "grace" or by sheer hard work that a man succeeds in transcending re- actions of hatred, feelings of aversion, of resentment?

E· That's not easy to answer. I know that one can achieve it by hard work, work of a spiritual kind; let us say: by a method, in the ascetic sense of the word. But "grace" does undoubtedly play an important part.

·R· Were you born with a nature that made such feelings easy for you? Or did you have to struggle to achieve serenity in the face of aggression?

·E· I think I struggled—very hard! Well, for me it was very hard. For others, for a saint, it would have been noth- ing at all, perhaps. But the important thing is that such efforts do produce results. They enrich you, and the conse- quences are there: you have become different.

·R· But what was your reason for struggling against the natural reaction, which is to hit back?

·E· The first, perhaps, was the feeling that when I followed my instincts I was—as the Hindus so accurately put it—a slave. I felt I was just the effect of a cause, whether physiological, psychological, or social. That made me rebel, naturally perhaps, against that conditioning. To be con- ditioned, when you become conscious of it, makes you angry. And so, in order to "decondition" myself, I had to do exactly the opposite of what karma was imposing on me. I had to break the cycle of cause and effect.

Animus and Anima

·R· You are a man of science, and your science is the science of myths. You are also a novelist, in other words an inventor of stories, a creator of imaginary worlds. On sev- eral occasions your *Journal* reveals the conflict between those two men inside you. Certain difficulties were of an external kind: in the early days, in Romania, your fame as a

171

been writing in the afternoon. I work at night, but I don't write. Except, of course, when I'm "possessed." Then it's day and night.

·R·   As a general rule, are you careful about using your time to the full?

·E·   I was very strict with myself when I was young. Every morning I reviewed the work ahead, laid out a program: so many hours learning a new language, so many finishing a book. Today it's slightly different.

·R·   When you're starting on a novel, how do you set about it?

·E·   I'm incapable of planning a novel. The germ of the book is always a vision, a landscape, or a dialogue. I can see the beginning very clearly, sometimes the end as well, and little by little, as I work on it, the incidents and the plot of the story or novel gradually come to me. With *The Forbidden Forest* the first image was of the central character. He was walking in a forest near Bucharest, an hour before midnight on Midsummer's Eve. He passes an automobile in the forest, then he sees a girl without an automobile. To me, that was an enigma. Who was the girl? And why should the man walking in the wood have been looking for an automobile and, nearby, a girl? Gradually I found out who the girl was, and her whole story. But it all began with a sort of vision. I saw it as in a dream.

·R·   But how did you know that your vision had a future?

·E·   I had no choice but to keep thinking about it, trying to see what came next. I was working on my book on shamanism at the time, but I had to abandon it and just set to, writing day and night. Other images appeared. The girl. The story that the young man was carrying inside him, which I didn't know but which fascinated me. His "secret room" in a hotel. And what happened that Midsummer Night.

·R·   Midsummer Night .... On 5 July 1949, you

wrote: "I suddenly remember that it was exactly twenty years ago, in the stifling heat of Calcutta, that I was writing the chapter 'Midsummer Night's Dream' in *Isabelle*. The same solstitial dream, differently structured, unfolding on other levels, also occurs at the center of *Noaptea de Sânziene* (*The Forbidden Forest*). Could that be pure coincidence? The myth and the symbol of the solstice have obsessed me for years. Yet I had forgotten that they have been pursuing me ever since *Isabelle*."

·E· It wasn't just the religious symbolism of the solstice that interested me but the images and themes of Romanian and European folklore that are associated with it: that night the sky opens; you can see beyond it, you can even disappear. If someone has that miraculous vision, he steps out of time, out of space. He lives through an instant that lasts an eternity. And yet, it isn't the meaning of that symbolism that was obsessing me, it was the night itself, always there.

·R· Midsummer Night is the year's great division: the days stop lengthening and begin to grow shorter. It is a central point. And then, at the end of the book, the first lines of the Divine Comedy return: *Nel mezzo del cammin di nostra vita, Mi ritrovai per una selva oscura.* What connection do you make between the summer solstice, the median line of life, and that initial forest vision? And what relation is there between the theme of the half and the theme of the double: the two "twin" characters, and the two women between whom the hero wavers?

·E· The forest in which Stéphane loses himself is the same one in which Dante found himself. He loses himself in it, or rather he passes through into another world of meaning while still remaining in history. It is the middle of time: the time of year and the time of his life. The dividing line between the historical world and the other. As for the theme of the double.... Stéphane is obsessed by this question: can one love two women at the same time with the same kind of love? He feels very strongly that it is impossible for man as we know him. But he is also obsessed by the existence of a world in which our limitations would be transcended. He is perfectly aware that he is no saint, not even a religious person, but he often thinks about saintliness: saints are men capable of loving *everyone at the same time.* That explains the presence of the two women. But I find it hard to answer your question about the two male characters. A psychoanalyst, Doctor Laforgue, regarded the death of the "double," for which Stéphane is indirectly responsible, as fraught with meaning. All I can say myself is that I invented the "double" in order to add density to the linear, epic plot. Stéphane had to exist in his wife's thoughts before he met her.

·R· Is it an important question for you—whether one can love two or more people simultaneously?

·E· Not personally. What interested me was the notion of going beyond our everyday limitations. If such an experience is possible, then it means that the human condition can be transcended. And in our modern, profane world, anyone can dream of loving two women. So I chose that situation because it's a notion that anyone can grasp.

·R· It is the dream of a whole section of American youth: abandoning monogamy.

·E· At the lowest level it represents a certain nostalgia for Eden, a desire to abolish the laws and structures inherent in every society; to abolish them in order to live in an Edenic state. But it is true that the hippies too, like Stéphane, wanted to transcend the conditions of everyday existence.

·R· Which is the road to paradise, or happiness: plural love, or single love, the great passion?

·E· I'd say that it is the great passion, love for a single person, that enriches the spirit and the emotions.

·R· You have traveled through so many continents of the mind and spirit, observed so many different ways of life. Does it seem to you that the best path for men and women lies in monogamy?

176

·E· One can love several people in succession but not at the same time. One can make love: that's something different . . . .

·R· To love two people, love them *at the same time:* in other words, to change not only love but time as well. Your novel ends with these words: "He had realized that this final moment, infinite in its duration, would suffice him." That echoes the miraculous moment of Midsummer Night. And your novel refers back, beyond historical time, to a cosmic time, a time that the esoteric tradition calls the Great Year.

·E· Yes, the twelve thousand years that, in this case, become the twelve years between 1936 and 1948. It was my ambition to write a little *War and Peace.* But what I wanted was to depict, within that historical space of time, an ordinary man—a married civil servant, with a child—who is at the same time obsessed by a strange longing: being able to love two women at the same time, to have a secret room. I wanted to reconcile a certain historical "realism" with this aspiration to an extramundane mode of being, expressed in a character who is neither a philosopher nor a poet, not even a religious man. And that presented me with some very difficult problems. But that was what fascinated me.

·R· So that, underneath the ordinary, profane story of a young Romanian, living in the thirties, we have to decipher a destiny full of meaning and figures. As though, beneath the surface appearance, our lives rest upon some secret ordering of things.

·E· In my stories I always try to camouflage the fantastic within the everyday. In this novel, which observes all the rules of the "novelistic" novel—in other words, of the nineteenth-century novel—I tried to express a certain symbolic meaning of the human condition but in camouflaged form. The camouflage is successful, I think, since the symbolism doesn't in any way harm the epic line of the narrative. I believe that the transhistorical is always there, concealed within the historical, the extraordinary within the ordinary. Aldous Huxley wrote of the vision conferred by LSD as a *visio beatifica:* it enabled him to see forms and

177

colors as Van Gogh saw his famous chair. It is beyond doubt that this gray reality, this everyday life of ours, is a camouflage for something else. That is my deep conviction. One must try to recapture that in the "novelistic" novel too, not just in the fantastic novel or story.

·R· I know that you're not very fond of science fiction. Do you not see it as coming into the category of the "fantastic"? In your *Journal* you predict a future for literature in the fantastic vein, because it can give back to modern man his taste for meaning. What exactly is your relationship with the "fantastic"?

·E· In all of my stories the narrative progresses on several levels, in order to achieve a gradual revelation of the "fantastic" that is concealed beneath everyday banality. Just as a new scientific axiom reveals a hitherto unknown structure of reality—in other words, provides the *foundation* of a new world—so fantastic literature reveals, or rather creates, parallel universes. It is not a matter of escapism, as certain critics think, because *creation*—at every level and in every sense of the word—is the specific characteristic of the human condition.

Writing One's Life

·R· In your *Journal* you make it plain that you are very much attracted to private diaries, intimate journals—those of Julien Green, for example, or Charles du Bos.

·E· Yes, I like private diaries very much. I like eavesdropping on the moment-by-moment experiences that their writers have caught on the wing. That passion for salvaging time is also the reason why I keep my own journal. To preserve fleeting moments by noting them down, briefly—or even at some length. Even so, you need to have the gift for it, like Jules Renard, Gide, Jünger, Green. Mere "notebooks" don't make a real diary.

·R· What spurred you on to publish extracts from your journal?

·E· I wanted to preserve at least some part of it. It

consists of a bundle of exercise books, which I carry around with me and have on occasion lost. And besides, there were a number of useful observations there—plans, projects. I felt that I'd never have the time to write even an essay on those topics. Publishing the journal was my way of passing on those few observations, those notes, and initiating a dialogue.

·R·   You are a very reserved, very reticent person, if not actually secretive. Wasn't it a problem for you, at all, to exhibit yourself in that way? Was it perhaps a kind of ordeal you put yourself through, like the one Saint Francis of Assisi imposed on his disciples when he made them walk naked through the city? Was there anything "sacrificial" in the act of publication? And was it perhaps your preparation for another "birth"?

·E·   Yes, it was a "sacrificial" act. I gauged the risk, even the danger. But I needed to stop camouflaging my oneiric, artistic side. And I wanted to oppose that academic superstition, which is still alive in Anglo-Saxon countries and even in the United States, which consists in a tendency to depreciate the act of literary imagination. As though a spontaneous, free creation is valueless in comparison with a purely scientific procedure. It's a very damaging superstition. I remember Bronowski, one of the greatest philosophers of science, writing that the process by which one discovers a new axiom can never be mechanized. "It is a free play of the mind, an invention outside the logical processes. That is the central act of imagination in science. And it is in all respects like any similar act in literature." Bronowski wrote that in "The Logic of the Mind," published in *The American Scientist* in spring 1966. So modern science discovered the value of imagination in the acquisition of knowledge a long while ago. And I rebel against this so-called scientific positivism of academics who claim that literary creation is no more than a game, unconnected with cognitive activity. I believe just the opposite.

·R·   Your *Journal* was warmly received, wasn't it?

·E·   Yes, it was. I received quite a number of letters

from people teaching English literature or comparative literature. They said: "In the past, your books on symbolism have been a help to me in my literary hermeneutics. I have now read your *Journal,* and I was astonished to meet the man who produced those tools I have been using. I discovered that he is someone who is also a writer, someone involved in literary activity himself." Publishing my journal helped me to achieve a new relationship with my readers, one that has brought me great pleasure. I wasn't expecting that.

·R· Somewhere in the *Journal* you write that "what I ought to write now, at all costs, leaving all other work aside, is my autobiography." Is that autobiography still unfinished?

·E· Yes, it breaks off at the outbreak of the Second World War. The first part has been published in Romanian, though not in Romania. The second part, aside from a few fragments, is still unpublished. I wrote it to bear witness. I lived through the period that is now referred to in Romania as the "prerevolutionary" or "bourgeois" period, and in reading certain articles, and even books, I realized that it was being distorted, because only its negative aspects were being shown. So I wanted to tell my own story: my experiences at school, at high school. As objectively as possible. Apart from which, it deals with a time long past, and with people who are no longer with us: Dasgupta, Tagore, Ortega . . . . In other words, I wrote it out of a sense of personal duty. For my friends in the future.

The Old Man and the Bureaucrats

·R· In your *Journal* you say that *The Old Man and the Bureaucrats* is the freest work you have written.

·E· Yes, because I wrote it as it came, like *The Serpent,* though without a deadline in this case. I wrote almost all of it in two or three weeks, and then I spent twelve years vainly attempting to write the last twenty-five pages. I finally managed it at a time when I was in fact very busy teaching at the University of Chicago and entertaining visiting guests. It took me four or five nights.

·R· It's a work you're very attached to.

·E· Everyone agrees that it's my most successful. I'm told that my Romanian is more subtle than in my other novels. And yet I wrote it after being in exile for twenty years—twenty years in which I have spoken Romanian only with my wife and friends. But I'm attached to it for other reasons as well.

·R· Ought we to give a summary of the plot, to start with?

·E· You do it for me: you've just reread it.

·R· Right. So we are in Romania—in other words, a police state. An old man, a former headmaster, tries to look up someone who had been a pupil of his thirty years earlier. But the man he meets isn't his former student—just someone with the same name. The misunderstandings that result arouse suspicion, and the police arrest the old man in order to find out more about him. Docilely, very politely, the old man tells them everything. He tells them his stories, which are fabulous—very long and labyrinthine. "It's a long story," he is constantly saying, "and if you're to understand it, I must first tell you. . . ." And the amazing thing is, they listen. He is even told to take his time and write his stories down. As he does so, the manuscript is removed, read, and analyzed, and the old man gets to meet increasingly important people, right up to a very close woman friend of the minister of the interior. (These stories of his have been described as "the *Arabian Nights* in a Stalinist world.") And as the fantastic narrative proliferates, the inquiry provokes palace revolutions. That is the main plot. But it must be said that the reader, like the police, is seduced, held spellbound. There is a flooded cellar into which a rabbi's son disappears: the cellar is drained, and he has vanished. There is an arrow that is shot into the air but never falls to earth. And the girl giant, as beautiful as a statue and doomed to extraordinary

181

love affairs: she reminds me of a character in one of your stories, *Le Macranthrope:* the man who grows and grows until he becomes a giant, but it isn't only his size that changes; his nature does, too. He can hear the gods. What do they say? We, down below, can no longer understand the sounds that emerge from his mouth. Well, there is this girl giant, there are the conjurors who shut up a village band, and indeed the whole village, in a box. We are in the inexhaustible universe of the old, old stories that can still cast their spell on us.

·E·   Yes, that's right.

·R·   But what does it all mean? Beyond the enchantment, we are being invited to seek for a meaning. We have the feeling that we are in the presence of a parable, in the sense in which Claudel saw Kafka as the great inventor of parables for our time.

·E·   I wanted to engineer a confrontation between two mythologies: the mythology of folklore, of the people, which is still alive, still welling up in the old man, and the mythology of the modern world, of technocracy. And that goes far beyond just the police in a totalitarian state; it is the mythology of people armed with logic and every kind of technical equipment. These two mythologies meet head on. The police try to decipher the hidden meaning of all these stories. And in a sense they are right to do so. But they are so blinkered they can only look for political secrets. Such people try to decipher the other universe—the other mythology—in terms of their own mythology. They are incapable of imagining that there can be any meaning outside the political field.

     The novel is equally a parable of man's fragility. The old man's name, Farâma, is Romanian for "crumb" or "fragment." Yet it is he who survives and the great and powerful who fall. Which means, if nothing else, that the man who can tell stories is capable, in certain difficult circumstances, of saving himself. That is what has happened, in fact, in Russian concentration camps. More people have survived in the barracks that are lucky enough to have a storyteller in them than in those that don't. Listening to

182

stories has helped them to live through the hell of their imprisonment.

·R· It seems to me that the old man also signifies something else. He says, almost in so many words: "I am childhood." In alchemy, the old man and the sun child both signify perfection, don't they? And the oldest is the man who remembers the beginning? And God is at the same time the Ancient of Days and the Divine Child. I see your old man as a personification of time, or rather of memory.

·E· Yes, he is *puer-senex:* child and old man at the same time. *Puer-senex* and *puer-aeternus:* the eternal child, the eternally "reborn." I think you've done an excellent piece of code-cracking, of exegesis, there. Yes, he is memory.

·R· "Think back," Farâma says. And men remember themselves. Along the paths of fable, of childhood, they re-discover their truth. The old man calls back a time that was, the time of primary school, thirty years before, and that act of recollection is sufficient to ensure that, from another, deeper level, legendary time is conjured up too. In short: beneath history is myth and, beneath myth, the memory of the world's origin. Is that it?

·E· I agree with your interpretation totally. You have touched bottom there, I think.

·R· In *Myth and Reality,* in the chapter "Mythologies of Memory and Forgetting," you say that "true historio-graphical anamnesis likewise leads us back to a primordial Time, the Time when men laid the foundations of their cultural behavior while believing that that behavior was re-vealed to them by supernatural beings." I also see your novel as an allegory of the historian of religions restoring memory to a forgetful mankind and saving them in the process. Which means that every memory is also a memory of the world's origin, and every memory of that origin is light and salvation. Because nothing is lost; because, thanks to time—to time's inextricably linked powers of destruction and creation—that origin has acquired meaning. In that case,

183

it is easy to see why history finds its fulfillment in hermeneutics, and hermeneutics in creation, in poetry. It seems to me that Zaharia Farâma is the mythic twin, the brother and the double of Mircea Eliade.

·E·   That is beautifully put. There is nothing more to be said.

The Meaning of the Labyrinth

·R·   You have often compared life—your life—to a
labyrinth. What would you say, today, about the meaning of
that labyrinth?

·E·   A labyrinth is a defense, sometimes a magical defense, built to guard a center, a treasure, a meaning. Entering it can be a rite of initiation, as we see in the Theseus
myth. That symbolism is the model of all existence, which
passes through many ordeals in order to journey toward its
own center, toward itself, toward *ātman,* as the Hindus call
it. There have been occasions when I have been aware of
emerging from a labyrinth, or of coming across the thread. I
was feeling hopeless, oppressed, lost. Of course I didn't actually say to myself: "I am lost in the labyrinth." And yet, in
the end, I did very much have the feeling of having emerged
from a labyrinth as a victor. Everyone has had that experience. But one must also add that life is not just *one*
labyrinth. The trial, the ordeal, recurs.

·R·   Have you reached your center?

·E·   Several times I have felt certain I was touching it,
and in doing so I learned a great deal, I recognized myself.
And then I lost myself again. That is our condition: we are
neither angels nor pure heroes. Once the center has been
reached, we are enriched, our consciousness is broadened and
deepened, so that everything becomes clear, meaningful;
but life goes on: another labyrinth, other encounters, other

kinds of trials, on another level. These conversations of ours, for example, have led me into a kind of labyrinth.

·R·   You spoke just now of moments when you "recognized" yourself. That makes me think of what the Sufi tradition says, or Zen: that man is invited to contemplate the face he had before he was born or the angel that he is in secret. What was your face like when you recognized yourself? Do you prefer to remain silent on that point?

·E·   Yes.

·R·   In your *Journal* you describe the sudden awareness you had one day of the duration of your life, of its continuity and its depth.

·E·   It's an experience I've had several times, one that is very important when you want to find yourself again, to get through to the meaning of your existence. In general we live our lives in segments. One day, in Chicago, as I was walking past the Oriental Institute, I became aware of the continuity underlying all that period that began with my adolescence and then took me on to India, to London, and all the other places. It is a comforting experience: you feel you haven't lost all that time, wasted your life. Everything is still there, even the times you thought were unimportant and had forgotten, like my military service, for example. Everything is still there, and you can see that there is a goal to guide us—an *orientatio.*

·R·   And there was nothing in it that was bad?

·E·   I can see a fair number of mistakes, or inadequacies—of failures too, perhaps. But bad? To be honest, no. But possibly I won't allow myself to see it.

·R·   How do you view your work as a whole today?

·E·   I flatter myself I'm still in the thick of it. There are still a great many things I have to do. But if anyone wants to judge what I've written up till now, then my books should be viewed as a whole. If there is any value, any significance

186

there, then it is from the work as a whole that it will emerge. After all, Balzac is not *Le Père Goriot,* or *Le Cousin Pons,* admirable as those works are; he is *La Comédie humaine.* And it is Goethe's whole work, not just *Faust,* that gives us the meaning of Goethe. In the same way, if I dare to compare myself just for one instant with those giants, it is only the totality of my writings that can reveal the meaning of my work. I envy those writers who fulfill themselves in a single great poem or great novel. I envy not only the genius of a Rimbaud or a Mallarmé but also that of Flaubert, for example: he is there in his entirety in *L'Education sentimentale.* Unfortunately for me, however, I have never managed to write a book that represents me totally. Some of my books are doubtless better written, more compact, clearer than others; and there are others that no doubt suffer from repetitions and are possible semi-failures. But, I say it again, no one can grasp the meaning of my life and what I have done except from the whole. And that's no easy task. Some of my books are written in Romanian and are therefore inaccessible in the West; the rest are written in French and are still inaccessible in Romania.

·R· Do you think these *Conversations* may be of help in achieving such an eagle's-eye view?

·E· I have encountered obstacles in the course of them, not only of language but also of an inner kind. I have relived, unexpectedly, certain important moments of my life, of my youth. Your questions have sometimes forced me to rethink certain problems. In a way, you have forced me to recall large areas of my life. Too large, perhaps? That is the danger . . . . One can't go deeply into everything one says. At all events, I shall be interested to read them when they have been transcribed. I recognize myself in advance in all that I have said—questions of form aside—but on condition that I'm allowed to stress one point: I don't feel I've answered you in a perfectly clear and definitive way. The things I have said should be taken for what they are: provisional answers, conditioned by circumstance. Everything remains open. All the questions might need answering

187

again. The answers I have given are true, but partial. I could still add things, stress different things. It is in the nature of such dialogues. I believe Ionesco felt the same after a similar series of conversations. Yes, everything is still open. And, as one does after any unexpected experience, I find my outlook has changed, broadened, to include new and unfamiliar things. I now find myself thinking extremely interesting things, things that wouldn't have occurred to me a few weeks ago. When I began these conversations, I knew that I had certain things to say, but they aren't what come to my mind today. The future opening up: that is the image haunting me now.

·R·   It must have taken great strength to accomplish all the work you have produced in your lifetime. Where does that strength come from? Do you know, deep down, what spurred you on to create so much?

·E·   I don't know what to answer. . . . Let us say: destiny.

·R·   I have constantly put off asking you about the divine, sensing your reticence in advance.

·E·   It is true that certain questions are of such importance for my very existence, and for any reader who is deeply concerned with them, that it would not be fitting to broach them in conversation. The question of divinity, central as it is, is one I would not wish to let myself speak of lightly. But I do hope to tackle it one day, in a completely personal and coherent way, in writing.

·R·   Is that silence also partly the result of your refusal to play the role of spiritual teacher?

·E·   It's certainly true that I don't regard myself as a spiritual teacher or guru. I feel that I am not even a guide, only a companion—a companion slightly further along the road, a companion to those who travel with me. And that is why, again, I hesitate to tackle certain essential problems in an impromptu way. I know what I believe, but it can't be said in so many words.

·R· You have often talked about the *real*.

·E· Yes.

·R· What is the *real* for you? What is real?

·E· Can one define it just like that? I can't define it. It seems self-evident to me; and if it isn't self-evident, then it would doubtless require a long proof.

·R· Doesn't Saint Augustine come to your help here? "If a man asks me what being is, I don't know; if he doesn't ask me . . . ."

·E· " . . . then I know." Yes, that is really the best answer.

Appendixes

Brancusi and Mythology

I have recently been rereading the fascinating documents that make up the controversy surrounding Brancusi: did he remain a "Carpathian peasant" despite having lived for half a century in Paris, at the very heart of all the innovations and revolutions of modern art? Or, on the contrary—as the American critic Sidney Geist thinks, for example—did Brancusi become what he was as the result of influences exerted on him by the School of Paris and the discovery of exotic art forms—above all, the discovery of African masks and sculpture?

As I read these documents, I looked at the photographs, reproduced by Ionel Jianou in his monograph (Paris: Arted, 1963), showing Brancusi in his studio on the Impasse Ronsin, his bed, his stove. It is difficult not to recognize in them the "style" of a peasant dwelling. And yet there is something else there too: one is seeing Brancusi's *abode,* his very own "world," which he had forged all by himself, with his own hands, one might almost say. It is not a replica of any preexisting model, whether "Romanian peasant dwelling" or "avant-garde Parisian artist's studio."

And then, one only needs to take a really good look at that stove. Not only because the need to have a peasant stove tells us a lot about the way of life Brancusi

This essay first appeared in *Témoignages sur Brancusi,* by Petru Comarnesco, Mircea Eliade, and Ionel Jianou, in the series Editions d'Art (Paris: Arted, 1967).

193

chose to retain in Paris, but also because the symbolism of the stove or hearth can illuminate a certain secret of Brancusi's genius.

There is, indubitably, this fact—a paradoxical one for many critics—that Brancusi seems to have rediscovered a "Romanian" source of inspiration after his encounter with certain "primitive" archaic artistic creations.

Now this "paradox" constitutes one of the favorite themes of folk wisdom. I shall limit myself to a single example here: the story of Rabbi Eisik of Cracow, which the Indianist Heinrich Zimmer took from Martin Buber's *Tales of the Hasidim*. This pious rabbi, Eisik of Cracow, had a dream telling him to go to Prague, where, beneath the great bridge leading to the royal castle, he would find a buried treasure. The dream recurred three times, and the rabbi resolved to make the journey. He arrived in Prague and found the bridge, but it was guarded night and day by sentries, so that Eisik didn't dare to dig beneath it. His constant prowling finally drew the attention of the captain of the guard, who asked him in a friendly way if he had lost something. The rabbi, a simple man, recounted his dream. The officer burst out laughing: "Really, my poor chap," he said to the rabbi, "you haven't actually worn out all that shoe leather coming here simply on account of a dream, have you? What rational person would believe in a dream?" The officer too had heard a voice in a dream: "It went on about Cracow, telling me to go there and look for a great treasure in the house of a rabbi called Eisik, Eisik son of Jekel. I was supposed to find this treasure hidden in a dusty recess behind the stove." But the officer put no faith in dream voices; the officer was a rational man. The rabbi bowed very low, thanked him, and hurried back to Cracow. He searched in the walled-up recess behind his stove and uncovered the treasure that put an end to his poverty.

"And so," Heinrich Zimmer comments, "the real treasure, the treasure that brings our wretchedness and our ordeals to an end, is never far away. We must never go looking for it in distant lands, for it lies buried in the most secret recesses of our own house; in other words, of our own being.

It is behind the stove, the life- and heat-giving center that governs our existence, the heart of our hearth, if only we know how to dig for it. But then there is the strange and constant fact that it is only after a pious journey to a distant region, in a strange land, a new country, that the meaning of the inner voice guiding our search can be revealed to us. And added to that strange and constant fact there is another: that the person who reveals the meaning of our mysterious inner voyage to us must himself be a stranger, of another faith and another race."

To return to our subject: even if we accept Sidney Geist's view—in particular, that the influence exerted by the School of Paris was decisive in Brancusi's formation and that "the influence of Romanian folk art was nonexistent"—the fact remains that Brancusi's masterpieces are an extension of the world of Romanian folk mythology and its plastic forms and sometimes even have Romanian names, as in the case of the *Maïastra,* for example. In other words, Geist's "influences" must have produced a kind of anamnesis that led ineluctably to a process of self-discovery. Brancusi's encounters with the creations of the Parisian avant-garde and those of the archaic world (Africa) triggered a process of "interiorization," a journey back toward a world that was both secret and unforgettable because it was simultaneously that of childhood and that of the imagination. Perhaps it was indeed *after* he had realized the importance of certain modern creations that Brancusi rediscovered the artistic richness of his own peasant tradition; that he divined, in short, the creative possibilities of that tradition. In either case, however, what Brancusi certainly did not do, having made that discovery, was to settle down to producing "Romanian folk art." He didn't imitate already-existing forms; he didn't make copies of traditional folk artworks. On the contrary, he understood that the source of all those forms—those of his own country's folk art as well as those of Balkan and Mediterranean protohistory and of "primitive" African or Oceanian art—was very deeply buried in the past; and he understood equally that this primordial source bore no relation to the "classical" history of sculpture in which he had been situated, like all his contemporaries, during his youth in Bucharest, Munich, and Paris.

Brancusi's genius stems from the fact that he knew where to look for the true "source" of the forms he felt himself capable of creating. Instead of reproducing the plastic worlds of Romanian or African folk art, he set himself to "interiorizing," as it were, his own vital experience. So that he succeeded in rediscovering the "presence-in-the-world" specific to archaic man, whether Lower Paleolithic hunter or Mediterranean, Carpatho-Danubian, or African Neolithic cultivator. If people have been able to perceive in Brancusi's work not only a structural and morphological solidarity with Romanian folk art but also analogies with Black African art and with the sculpture of Mediterranean and Balkan prehistory, that is because all those plastic universes can be regarded as culturally homologous: their sources are all to be found in the Lower Paleolithic and the Neolithic. In other words, thanks to the process of "interiorization," already referred to, and the anamnesis that followed it, Brancusi succeeded in "seeing the world" in the same way as the creators of prehistoric, ethnic, or folk-art masterpieces. He rediscovered, in a way, the presence-in-the-world that enabled those anonymous artists to create their own plastic universe within a space that had nothing whatever to do with, for example, the space of classical Greek art.

All this does not, of course, "explain" Brancusi's genius or his work. It is not enough to rediscover the presence-in-the-world of a Neolithic peasant to be able to create like an artist of that period. But drawing attention to this process of "interiorization" does help us to understand, first, Brancusi's startling originality and, second, why certain of his works appear to be structurally akin to peasant, ethnic, or prehistoric artistic productions.

Brancusi's attitude toward his materials, and especially toward stone, may possibly help us one day to understand something about the mentality of prehistoric man. For Brancusi addressed himself to certain stones with the awed and ecstatic reverence of someone for whom such an object was the manifestation of a sacred power and was thus, in itself, a sacred mystery.

196

We shall never know in what imaginative universe Brancusi was moving during his long polishing process. But that prolonged intimacy with the stone undoubtedly favored the "material reveries" so brilliantly analyzed by Gaston Bachelard. It was a sort of immersion in a deeply buried world where stone, the most "material" form of matter we have, revealed itself as a thing of mystery, since it embodies and conceals sacrality, energy, and chance. In discovering "matter" as a source and locus of epiphanies and religious meanings, Brancusi was able to rediscover, or divine, the emotions and the inspiration of the artist of archaic times.

Moreover, "interiorization" and "immersion" in the depths both formed part of the early twentieth-century *Zeitgeist.* Freud had just developed his technique for exploring the deeps of the unconscious; Jung believed in the possibility of penetrating even more deeply, down to what he called the collective unconscious; the speleologist Emile Racovitza was in the process of identifying "living fossils" among the subterranean fauna, organic forms made all the more precious by the fact that they are no longer fossilizable; Lévy-Bruhl was isolating his "primitive mentality," an archaic, prelogical phase in the development of human thought.

All these researches and discoveries had one thing in common: they were revealing values, states, or forms of behavior hitherto unknown to science, either because they had previously been inaccessible to research or, above all, because they had offered nothing of interest to the rationalistic mentality of the second half of the nineteenth century. All these researches implied some sort of *descensus ad inferos* and, as a consequence, the discovery of phases of life, experience, and thought that preceded the formation of those systems of meaning known and studied up till then, the systems that one might term "classical," since they were all, in one way or another, connected with the establishment of reason as the sole principle capable of apprehending reality.

Brancusi was eminently a *contemporary* of this tendency toward "interiorization" and exploration of the "depths," a *contemporary* of this passionate interest in the primitive, prehistoric, and prerational stage of human creativity. Having grasped the central "secret"—that it is not the creations of ethnic or folk art in themselves that will enable us to renew and enrich modern art but rather the discovery of their "sources"—Brancusi threw himself into an endless quest that was terminated only by his death. He returned indefatigably to certain themes, as though obsessed by their mystery or their artistic possibilities, which he never completely succeeded in realizing. For example, he worked for nineteen years on the *Colonne sans fin* and for twenty-eight on the *Birds* cycle. Ionel Jianou, in his *Catalogue raisonné*, lists five versions of the *Colonne sans fin* in oak plus one in plaster and steel, all made between 1918 and 1937. As for the *Birds* cycle, Brancusi completed twenty-nine versions of that between 1912 and 1940, some in polished bronze, some in marble of various colors, some in plaster. It is true, of course, that the constant reiteration of a particular central motif is also found in the work of other artists, ancient and modern. But such a method is characteristic above all of folk and ethnographic arts, in which the exemplary models must be indefinitely reworked and "imitated" for reasons that have nothing to do with "lack of imagination" or the artist's "personality."

It is significant that, in the *Colonne sans fin,* Brancusi should have rediscovered a Romanian folklore motif, the "pillar of the sky" (*columna cerului*), which is an extension of a mythological theme already shown to exist in prehistory, as well as being fairly widespread throughout the world. The "pillar of the sky" supports the heavenly vault. In other words, it is an *axis mundi,* the numerous variants of which are well known: Irminsul, the world pillar of the ancient Germans, the cosmic pillars of the North Asian peoples, the central mountain, the cosmic tree, and so on. The symbolism of the *axis mundi* is complex: the axis supports the sky and is also the means of communication between heaven and earth. When he is close to an *axis mundi,* which is regarded as the center of the world, man can communicate with the heavenly powers. The concept of the *axis mundi* as a stone column supporting the world very probably reflects beliefs characteristic of megalithic culture (four to three thousand years B.C.). But the symbolism and mythology of the sky pillar extend beyond the boundaries of megalithic culture.

In Romanian folklore, at all events, the "pillar of the sky" represents an archaic, pre-Christian belief but one that quickly became Christianized, since it is found in the ritual Christmas songs, or *colinde*. Brancusi would undoubtedly have heard about the sky pillar in the village where he was born, or in the Carpathians, where he served his apprenticeship as a shepherd. The image certainly obsessed him, for, as we shall see, it formed part of the symbolism of ascension, of flight, of transcendence. It is worth noting that Brancusi did not choose the "pure" form of the column—which could signify nothing more than the support, the "prop" of heaven—but a form consisting of repeated rhomboids, which make it akin to a tree or to a notched pole. In other words, Brancusi succeeded in bringing out the inherent symbolism of ascension, since one's imaginative response is a desire to climb this "tree of heaven." Ionel Jianou points out that the rhomboidal shapes "represent a decorative motif taken from the pillars of peasant architecture." And the symbolism of the pillar in peasant houses likewise derives from the "symbolic field" of the *axis mundi.* In many archaic dwellings the central pillar does in fact serve as a means of communication with the heavens, with the sky.

However, it is not the ascension to heaven of the archaic and primitive cosmologies that obsesses Brancusi but the sensation of flight out into infinite space. He calls his column "endless" not only because such a column could never reach a structural conclusion but above all because it hurls itself out into a space that must always remain without limits, since it is based on the ecstatic experience of absolute freedom. It is the same space in which his *Birds* fly. Brancusi has discarded everything from the old symbolism of the sky pillar except its central element: ascension as a transcendence of the human condition. But he successfully revealed to his contemporaries that what concerned him was an ecstatic ascension stripped of all mysticism. One need only allow oneself to be "carried away," lifted, by the power of the work to recover the forgotten bliss of an existence freed from any and every system of conditionings.

The theme of his *Birds* series, which began in 1912 with the first version of the *Maïastra,* is even more revealing. Taking a well-known motif from Romanian folklore as his starting point, Brancusi worked his way through a long process of "interiorization" toward a simultaneously archaic and universal exemplary theme. The Maïastra—or, more specifically, the Paserea Maïastra (literally "The Magic Bird")—is a fabulous bird that assists the Prince Charming (*Fat-Frumos*) of Romanian folktales in his combats and ordeals. In another narrative cycle the Maïastra succeeds in stealing the three golden apples that a magic apple tree produces every year. Only a king's son can wound or capture it. In some variants, once wounded or snared, the magic bird reverts to its true shape as a fairy. In his first version (1912–17) it is as though Brancusi wished to suggest this mystery in its double nature by emphasizing the Maïastra's femininity. Fairly soon, however, his interest becomes concentrated on the mystery of the bird's flight. Ionel Jianou has collated various statements made by Brancusi himself on this point: "I wanted the *Maïastra* to raise its head aloft without expressing either pride or defiance by that movement. That was the most difficult problem, and it was only after a long struggle that I succeeded in integrating that movement into the soaring movement of the bird's flight." The Maïastra, which in folklore is practically invulnerable—the Prince alone can wound it—then becomes *Bird in Space.* In other words, it is now its "magical flight" that Brancusi wants to express in stone. The first version of the *Maïastra* as *Bird in Space* dates from 1919, the last from 1940. In the end, as Jianou writes, Brancusi succeeded in "transforming his amorphous material into an ellipse with translucent surface, of a purity so dazzling that it irradiates the light around it and embodies, in its irresistible upward impulse, the very essence of flight."

Moreover, Brancusi himself said: "I have been searching a whole lifetime for only one thing: the essence of flight.... Flight, what happiness!" He did not need to read books to find out that flight is an equivalent of happiness because it symbolizes ascent, transcendence, a farewell to our human condition. Flight proclaims that *weight has been abolished,* that an ontological mutation has taken place within man's very being. Myths, tales, and legends relating to heroes or magicians who can move freely between earth and heaven are found everywhere in the world. A whole cluster of symbols bearing on the life of the spirit, and above all on ecstatic experiences and the powers of the mind, relies on images of birds, wings, and flight. The symbolism of flight expresses an escape from the universe of everyday experience, and the double intentionality of that escape is obvious: it is at the same time *transcendence* and *freedom* that one obtains by "flight."

This is not the place to repeat the analyses that I have offered elsewhere; but it is possible to show that on the different interdependent levels of dream, active imagination, mythological and folk creation, rituals, metaphysical speculation, and ecstatic experience, the symbolism of ascension always signifies the shattering of a "petrified" or "blocked" situation, the bursting-open of a "ceiling," a sudden possibility of transition to another mode of being and, ultimately, the freedom to "move," or, in other words, to change situations, to abolish a system of conditionings. It is significant that Brancusi was obsessed throughout his life with what he called "the essence of flight." But it is extraordinary that he succeeded in expressing that soaring, upward impulse by using the very archetype of *heaviness,* that ultimate form of "matter"—stone. One might almost say that he performed a transmutation of "matter" or, more precisely, that he brought about a *coincidentia oppositorum,* since he achieved in one and the same object a coincidence of matter and flight, of weight and its negation.

Mircea Eliade
June 1967
University of Chicago

A Chronology of
Mircea Eliade's Life

1907   9 March: Birth in Bucharest of Mircea Eliade, second son of Captain Gheorghe Eliade and Joana Stoenesco.

1913   October: Begins schooling at primary school at number 10 Strada Mântuleasa.

1917–25   Secondary education at Spiru-Haret high school.

1921   January: Publishes first article, "How I Found the Philosopher's Stone," in *Ziarul Stiintelor Populare.*

1921–23   Contributes to numerous magazines (*Ziarul Stiintelor Populare, Orizontul, Foaia Tinerimii, Lumea, Universul Literar, Adevarul Literar,* etc.): popularizations of entomology, history of alchemy, Orientalism, history of religions; impressions of travels in the Carpathians and on the Danube; stories; literary criticism.

1923–25   Learns Italian in order to read Papini and Vittorio Macchioro and English in order to read Max Müller and Frazer. Begins learning Hebrew from textbook by Mihalcescu, Persian from grammar by Italo Pizzi.

1924–25   Writes still unpublished autobiographical novel, *Romanul adolescentului miop.*

1925   October: Passes baccalaureate (high school) examination and enrolls in the literature and philosophy department of Bucharest University.

1926   January: Starts *Revista Universitara,* which is suppressed after its third number because of an excessively derogatory review of N. Iorga's *Essai d'histoire universelle.*

November: Becomes a regular contributor to the daily newspaper *Cuvântul* (The Word); for several years contributes at least two articles a week (portraits of writers and scientists; reviews of works in Oriental studies, philosophy, history of religions; travel impressions, etc.).

1927   March–April: First journey to Italy, where he meets Papini in Florence; E. Buonaiuti, A. Panzini, and G. Gentile in Rome; and V. Macchioro in Naples.

July–August: Travels to Austria and Switzerland.

1928   January: Writes *Gaudeamus,* a sequel to *Romanul adolescentului miop;* also still unpublished.

April–June: Stays in Rome, where he works on his degree thesis ("Italian Philosophy, from Marsilio Ficino to Giordano Bruno"). After reading *A History of Indian Philosophy,* Eliade writes to Professor Surendranath Dasgupta, expressing a desire to work with him at the University of Calcutta. He also writes to the Maharajah Manindra Chandra Nandy of Kassimbazar, who had been Dasgupta's patron when he was a student.

June: Returns to Bucharest via Naples, Athens, and Constantinople.

September: Receives encouraging reply from Dasgupta and from the Maharajah. Latter promises him a scholarship to support him during his stay in India.

October: Obtains philosophy degree.

20 November: Leaves for India.

25 November–5 December: Travels in Egypt.

17–20 December: Arrives in Colombo and visits Sri Lanka.

21 December: Arrives in Madras and meets Dasgupta.

26 December: Arrives in Calcutta and takes up residence in an Anglo–Indian boardinghouse at 82 Ripon Street.

1929   January–June: Attends Dasgupta's classes and
        works very hard at learning Sanskrit.
        March: Travels to Benares, Allahabad, Agra,
        Jaipur.
        July: Travels to Darjeeling and Sikkim.
        August: Finishes a novel, *Isabel si Apele Di-*
        avolului, published in Bucharest the following
        year.
        September–December: Dasgupta suggests he
        work with a pandit so that he will be able to talk
        in Sanskrit with Hindu monks.
1930   January–September: Goes to live with Dasgupta
        at 120 Bakulbagan Street in the Bhowanipore
        district. An hour of textual analysis every morning
        under Dasgupta's guidance (the commentary of
        Patañjali, the grammarian).
        February: Chooses subject for doctoral thesis:
        "Comparative History of Yoga Techniques."
        June–July: Dasgupta dictates his book on the
        philosophy of the Upanishads to Eliade.
        Publications of his first investigations into Indian
        philosophies and religions in *Revista de Filozofie*
        (Bucharest) and *Ricerche Religiose* (Rome).
        September: Quarrel with Dasgupta. Leaves Bho-
        wanipore for Hardwar in western Himalayas.
        October: Takes up residence in an *ashram* at
        Rishikesh, where he wears a *kutiar* and practices
        Yoga for six months under the guidance of Swami
        Shivananda.
        December: Visits yogins at Lakshmanjula and talks
        with pilgrims returning from Badrinath.
1931   January–March: Meditation and practice of Yoga.
        April: Returns to Calcutta.
        April–November: Works in library of the Asiatic
        Society of Bengal and becomes friendly with the
        librarian, Tibetanist Johan Van Manen. Begins
        writing doctoral thesis.
        December: Leaves for Bucharest to do military
        service.
1932   January–November: Military service in 1st

regiment of antiaircraft artillery, in Bucharest.
Begins translating the English text of his thesis
into Romanian.

1933   January: Enters the manuscript of *Maitreyi* in
competition for best unpublished novel.

March: *Maitreyi* wins first prize, is published in
May, and achieves great critical and popular success.

June: Receives Ph.D. degree. The university
committee advises him to publish his dissertation
in French. Begins looking for a translator who
knows English, Romanian, and some Sanskrit.

November: Is appointed assistant to Naë Ionesco,
professor of logic and metaphysics. Begins teaching, with a course on "The Problem of Evil in
Indian Philosophy."

1934   January: Marries Nina Mares and takes an apartment on the Boulevard Dinicu-Golescu. In order
to meet financial commitments, he does work for
several magazines and publishes four books: two
novels (*Intoarcerea din Rai* and *Lumina ce se stinge*),
a collection of articles (*Oceanography*), and a travel
book (*India*).

August: Stays in Berlin to put finishing touches on
his dissertation.

November: Begins teaching course on "Salvation
in Eastern Religions."

1935   Winter: Leads seminar on Nicolas de Cusa's *Docta
ignorantia.*

Spring: Publication of *Alchimia asiatica* and *San-
tier* (fictionalized excerpts from his Indian diary).

August: Goes back to Berlin for final work on
book about Babylonian cosmology and alchemy.

November: Begins his course entitled "The Upanishads and Buddhism."

1936   Winter: Seminar on Book X of Aristotle's
Metaphysics.

June: Works on a critical edition of selected
works of B. P. Hasdeu. Publication of *Yoga: Essai*

sur les origines de la mystique indienne (Paris and Bucharest: Paul Geuthner and Fundatia Regala Carol I).

July–August: Travels to London, Oxford, and Berlin.

1937   Teaches course on "Religious Symbolism." Publication of Hasdeu's selected writings in two volumes, and of *Cosmologie si alchimie babiloniana.*

Summer: Travels to Switzerland and Italy.

1938   Teaches course on "History of Buddhism." Works on first issue of *Zalmoxis: A Review of Religious Studies,* in collaboration with R. Pettazzoni, J. Przyluski, Ananda Coomaraswamy, Carl Clemen, C. Hentze, B. Rowland, et al.

November: Publication of *Nunta in Cer* (a novel).

1939   Spring: Publication of first issue of *Zalmoxis* (distributed by Paul Geuthner's Librairie orientaliste).

Summer: Works on second issue of *Zalmoxis,* which appears in 1940.

Autumn: Publication of *Fragmentarium* (essays).

1940   March: Is appointed cultural attaché to Romanian royal legation in London.

April–September: London.

September: Is evacuated to Oxford.

1941   January: Is appointed cultural adviser to Romanian royal legation in Lisbon.

10 February: Arrives in Lisbon, where he will remain until September 1945.

1942–44   Publication in Bucharest of four works in Romanian and third issue of *Zalmoxis.*

1943   Publishes *Os Romenos, Latinos do Oriente,* in Lisbon.

1944   November: Death of his wife, Nina.

December: Moves to Cascaes, a fishing village near Lisbon.

1945   Writes *Prolegomena to the History of Religions* in Romanian. (This work, begun in Oxford in 1940–41, was to appear in French in 1949 under the title *Traité d'histoire des religions* and was later translated into English as *Patterns in Comparative Religion*.)

September: Arrives in Paris with Nina's daughter, Adalgiza.

November: Is invited by Professor Georges Dumézil to give a course of lectures of his own choice at the Ecole des Hautes Etudes (uses first three chapters of the *Traité* [*Patterns*]).

December: Is elected to membership in the Société Asiatique.

1946–49 Lives in the Hôtel de Suède, rue Vaneau. Meets friends from Bucharest: E. M. Cioran, Eugène Ionesco, Nicolas Herescu. Contributes to *Critique, Revue de l'histoire des religions, Comprendre, Paru,* etc.

1947 Spring: Teaches course of his own choice at Ecole des Hautes Etudes (uses "The Myth of the Eternal Return").

1948 Spring: Gallimard publishes *Techniques du Yoga*.
June: Takes part in international congress of Orientalists in Paris.
Autumn: Starts *Luceafarul,* magazine for and by exiled Romanians.

1949 Winter: *Traité d'histoire des religions* is published in French.
Spring: *The Myth of the Eternal Return* is published in French (*Le Mythe d'Eternel Retour*).

1950 9 January: Marries Christinel Cottesco.
Spring: Travels to Italy with his wife.
March: Lectures at the University of Rome at invitation of professors R. Pettazzoni and G. Tucci.
August: Attends first Eranos Conference in Ascona, where he meets Jung, G. Van der Leeuw, Louis Massignon, et al.
September: Takes part in international congress on the history of religions in Amsterdam.

1951–55 Is given a research grant ($200 a month) by Bollingen Foundation of New York.

Doctor René Laforgue and Délia Laforgue, and Doctor Roger Godel and Alice Godel, invite the Eliades to live in their apartments in Paris and the Val-d'Or.

Becomes friendly with Henry Corbin, Father Jean Daniélou, R. P. Jean Bruno, Jean Gouillard, Luc Badesco, Christian and Marie-Louise Dehollain, Jacqueline Desjardin, Sibylle Cottesco, and the conductor Ionel Perlea and his wife Lisette.

Lectures at universities of Rome, Padua, Strasbourg, Munich, Freiburg, Lund, and Uppsala.

Principal publications: *Shamanism; Images and Symbols; Yoga; The Forge and the Crucible; The Forbidden Forest,* all in French—the last a novel translated from the Romanian manuscript by Alain Guillermou.

Takes part in congress on the history of religions in Rome.

1956   September: Leaves for the United States.

October–November: Gives Haskell Lectures at the University of Chicago: "Patterns of Initiation" (published in 1958 under the title *Rites and Symbols of Initiation: The Mysteries of Birth and Rebirth,* by Harper & Row. French translation, *Naissances mystiques,* 1959).

October–June 1957: Is visiting professor in the history of religions at Chicago.

1957   March: Accepts post of professor and chairman of the history of religions department and professor in the Committee on Social Thought at the University of Chicago.

1958   January: Begins teaching at the University of Chicago.

June: Returns to Paris.

August–September: Takes part, with his wife, in the international congress on the history of religions in Tokyo and travels in Japan with his colleague and friend Professor Joseph Kitagawa and his wife.

October: Returns to Chicago via Hawaii and San
Francisco.
Publication of four works in English translation:
Patterns in Comparative Religion (Traité); *Yoga;
Rites and Symbols of Initiation; The Sacred and the
Profane.*

1959   From now on teaches two semesters a year at
Chicago, supervises doctoral dissertations during
the third quarter, and spends the summer vacations in Europe.

1960   September: Takes part in the history of religions
congress in Marburg.

1961   Starts the journal *Antaios* with Ernst Jünger
(Stuttgart: Klett Verlag, 1961–72).

1963   Professor Thomas J. Altizer publishes *Mircea
Eliade and the Dialectics of the Sacred* (Philadelphia:
Westminster Press).

1964   The University of Chicago awards Eliade the title
of Sewell L. Avery Distinguished Service Professor.

1965   February–March: Travels to Mexico; gives lectures on Indian religions at the Collegio de
Mexico.

1966   May: Is elected to membership in the American
Academy of Arts and Sciences.
June: Receives Doctor Honoris Causa in
Humane Letters, Yale University.

1968   Receives Christian Culture Award, Gold Medal
for 1968, at the University of Windsor, Canada.

1969   Publication of *Myths and Symbols: Studies in Honor
of Mircea Eliade* (University of Chicago Press).
April–May: Travels to Argentina; gives lectures at
the Universidad de la Plata.
22 April: Receives Doctor Honoris Causa in
filosofia de las religiones, Universidad de la Plata.
7 May: Receives honorary title Professor Extra-
ordinario de la Escuela de Estudios Orientales at
the Universidad de San Salvador.
18 May: Receives Doctor Honoris Causa in Sa-

cred Theology, Ripon College, Ripon, Wisconsin.

1970   7 January: Receives Doctor Honoris Causa of Humane Letters, Loyola University (Chicago).
8 July: Is made a Corresponding Fellow of the British Academy.
August–September: Travels to Sweden and Norway. Takes part in international congress on the history of religions in Stockholm.

1971   June: Receives Doctor Honoris Causa in Science of Religion, Boston College.

1972   17 May: Receives Doctor Honoris Causa of Law, La Salle College, Philadelphia.
21 May: Receives Doctor of Humane Letters, Oberlin College.

1973   22 May: Is elected a corresponding member of the Austrian Academy of Sciences.
August: Travels to Finland; takes part in conference on the history of religions in Turku.
Autumn: Gallimard publishes *Fragments d'un Journal,* translated from the Romanian by Luc Badesco.

1974   Finishes first volume of *L'Histoire des croyances et des idées religieuses: De l'âge de la pierre aux mystères d'Eleusis,* which is published by Payot in 1976.

1975   16 August: Receives Doctor Honoris Causa of Letters, University of Lancaster, England.
September: Is elected member of the Royal Academy of Belgium.

1976   14 February: Receives Docteur Honoris Causa de l'Université de Paris–Sorbonne.

Bibliography:
Works by and about
Mircea Eliade

Works by Eliade

In English

*Autobiography: Volume 1. Journey East, Journey West, 1907–
1937.* Translated from the Romanian by Mac Linscott
Ricketts. New York: Harper & Row, 1981. (French edition: *Mémoire: I. Les Promesses de l'équinoxe, 1909–1937.*
Paris, 1980. Romanian edition: *Amintiri: I. Mansarda,
1907–1928.* Madrid, 1966.)

Australian Religions: An Introduction. Ithaca and London:
Cornell University Press, 1973.

*Birth and Rebirth: The Religious Meaning of Initiation in
Human Culture.* Translated by Willard R. Trask. New
York: Harper & Bros.; London: Harvill Press, 1958. Reprinted as *Rites and Symbols of Initiation.* New York:
Harper Torchbooks, 1965. (French edition: *Naissances
mystiques.* Paris, 1959. Reprinted, 1976, as *Initiation,
rites, sociétés secrètes.*)

Cosmos and History. See *The Myth of the Eternal Return.*

The Forbidden Forest. Novel. Translated by Mac Linscott
Ricketts and Mary Park Stevenson. Notre Dame: University of Notre Dame Press, 1978. (French edition: *Forêt
interdite.* Paris, 1955. Romanian edition: *Noaptea de Sânziene.* Paris, 1971.)

*The Forge and the Crucible: The Origins and Structures of
Alchemy.* Translated by Stephen Corrin. London: Ridder;
New York: Harper & Bros., 1962. (French edition:
Forgerons et alchimistes. Paris, 1956. 2d ed., enl., 1977.)

From Primitives to Zen: A Thematic Source Book on the History of Religions. London: Collins; New York: Harper and Row, 1967. Reprinted in 1974 in four volumes: *Gods, Goddesses, and Myths of Creation; Man and the Sacred; Death, Afterlife, and Eschatology;* and *From Medicine Man to Muhammad.*

A History of Religious Ideas. Translated by Willard R. Trask. Vol. 1: *From the Stone Age to the Eleusinian Mysteries.* Vol. 2: *From Gautama Buddha to the Triumph of Christianity.* Chicago: University of Chicago Press, 1978, 1982. (French edition: *Histoire des croyances et des idées religieuses.* 2 vols. Paris, 1976, 1978.) Volume 3, in preparation, will be entitled *From Muhammad to the Atheistic Theologies of the Present.*

Images and Symbols: Studies in Religious Symbolism. Translated by Philip Mairet. New York: Sheed & Ward; London: Harvill Press, 1961. (French edition: *Images et symboles: Essais sur le symbolisme magico-religieux.* Paris, 1952. Reprinted, 1965, 1970.)

Journal. See *No Souvenirs.*

Mephistopheles and the Androgyne: Studies in Religious Myth and Symbol. Translated by J. M. Cohen. New York: Sheed & Ward, 1965. Also published as *The Two and the One.* London: Harvill Press, 1965. (French edition: *Méphistophélès et l'Androgyne.* Paris, 1962. Reprinted, 1970.)

Metallurgy, Magic and Alchemy. Cahiers de Zalmoxis, no. 1. Paris: Librairie orientaliste Paul Geuthner, 1938.

"Midnight in Serampore." See *Two Tales of the Occult.*

The Myth of the Eternal Return. Translated by Willard R. Trask. New York: Pantheon, 1954. Reprinted, with new Preface, as *Cosmos and History.* New York: Harper Torchbooks, 1959. (French edition: *Le Mythe de l'éternel retour: Archétypes et répétition.* Paris, 1949. Reprinted, 1975.)

Myth and Reality. Translated by Willard R. Trask. New York: Harper & Row, 1963; London: Allen & Unwin, 1964. (French edition: *Aspects du mythe.* Paris, 1963. 2d ed., 1973.) ·

Myths, Dreams, and Mysteries. Translated by Philip Mairet.

New York: Harper & Bros.; London: Harvill Press, 1960. (French edition: *Mythes, rêves et mystères*. Paris, 1957. Reprinted, 1970.)

No Souvenirs: Journal, 1957–1969. Translated by Fred H. Johnson, Jr. New York: Harper & Row, 1977. (French edition: *Fragments d'un Journal, 1945–1969.* Paris, 1973.)

Occultism, Witchcraft, and Cultural Fashions: Essays in Comparative Religions. Chicago and London: University of Chicago Press, 1976.

The Old Man and the Bureaucrats. Translated by Mary Park Stevenson. Notre Dame and London: University of Notre Dame Press, 1979. (French edition: *Le Vieil homme et l'officier.* Paris, 1977. Romanian edition: *Pe Strada Mântuleasa* [Mântuleasa Street]. Paris, 1970.)

Patañjali and Yoga. Translated by Charles Markmann. New York: Funk & Wagnalls, 1969. (French edition: *Patañjali et le Yoga.* Paris, 1962. 2d rev. ed., 1976.)

Patterns in Comparative Religion. Translated by Rosemary Sheed. New York and London: Sheed & Ward, 1958. (French edition: *Traité d'histoire des religions.* Paris, 1949. 8th ed., 1975.)

The Quest: History and Meaning in Religion. Chicago and London: University of Chicago Press, 1969. (French edition: *La Nostalgie des origines: Méthodologie et histoire des religions.* Paris, 1971.)

Rites and Symbols of Initiation. See *Birth and Rebirth.*

The Sacred and the Profane: The Nature of Religion. Translated by Willard R. Trask. New York: Harcourt, Brace, 1959. (French edition: *Le Sacré et le profane.* Paris, 1956. Reprinted, 1975.)

"The Secret of Dr. Honigberger." See *Two Tales of the Occult.*

Shamanism: Archaic Techniques of Ecstasy. Translated by Willard R. Trask. Bollingen Series 76. New York: Pantheon, 1964. Princeton: Princeton University Press, 1972. (French edition: *Le Chamanisme et les techniques archaïques de l'extase.* Paris, 1951. 3d ed., rev. and enl., 1974.)

Tales of the Sacred and the Supernatural ("Les Trois Graces" and "With the Gypsy Girls"). Translated by Mac Linscott Ricketts and William Ames Coates. With a Foreword by Mircea Eliade. Philadelphia: Westminster Press, 1981.

The Two and the One. See *Mephistopheles and the Androgyne.*

Two Tales of the Occult ("Midnight in Serampore" and "The Secret of Dr. Honigberger"). Translated from the Romanian by William Ames Coates. New York: Herder & Herder, 1970. (French edition: *Minuit à Serampore.* Paris, 1956. Romanian edition: *Secretul Doctorului Honigberger* [includes "Nopti la Serampore"]. Bucharest, 1940.)

Yoga: Immortality and Freedom. Translated by Willard R. Trask. Bollingen Series 56. New York: Pantheon, 1958. Princeton: Princeton University Press, 1969. (French edition: *Le Yoga: Immortalité et liberté.* Paris, 1954. 5th ed., rev. and enl., 1975.)

Zalmoxis, the Vanishing God: Comparative Studies in the Religions and Folklore of Dacia and Eastern Europe. Translated by Willard R. Trask. Chicago: University of Chicago Press, 1972. (French edition: *De Zalmoxis à Gengis Khan.* Paris, 1970.)

French Works Not Translated into English

"Centre de monde, temple, maison." In R. Bloch, ed., *Le Symbolisme cosmique des monuments religieux.* Rome, 1957.

Fragments d'un Journal, 1970–1978. Paris, 1981.

Mademoiselle Christina (Miss Christina). Novel. Paris, 1978. (Romanian edition: *Domnisoara Christina.* Bucharest, 1936.)

La Nuit bengali (Bengal Night). Novel. Paris, 1950. 2d ed., Lausanne, 1966. (Romanian edition: *Maitreyi.* Bucharest, 1933.)

Le Serpent (The Serpent). Novel. Paris, 1978. (Romanian edition: *Sarpele.* Bucharest, 1937.)

Techniques du Yoga (Techniques of Yoga). Paris, 1936. 2d ed., rev. and enl., 1975.

Yoga: Essai sur les origines de la mystique indienne (Yoga: Essay on the Origins of Indian Mysticism). Paris, 1936.

Alchimia Asiatica (Asiatic Alchemy). Bucharest, 1934.
Comentarii la legenda Meşterului Manole (Commentaries on
the Legend of Master Manole). Bucharest, 1943.
Cosmologie şi Alchimie Babiloniană (Babylonian Cosmology
and Alchemy). Bucharest, 1937.
Fragmentarium. (Essays.) Bucharest, 1939.
Huliganii (The Hooligans). Novel. 2 vols. Bucharest, 1935.
In curte la Dionis (At the Court of Dionysus). Short stories.
Paris and Madrid, 1977.
India. Autobiographical work, covering the period 1929–
1933. Bucharest, 1934.
Insula lui Euthanasius (The Island of Euthanasius). Essays.
Bucharest, 1943.
Intoarcerea din Rai (The Return from Paradise). Novel.
Bucharest, 1934.
Intr'o mânăstire din Himalaya (In a Himalayan Monastery).
Autobiographical work. Bucharest, 1932.
Iphigenia. Drama. Valle Hermoso, 1951.
Isabel şi Apele Diavolului (Isabelle and the Devil's Waters).
Novel. Bucharest, 1930.
Lumina ce se stinge (The Light That Failed). Novel. Bucharest,
1934.
Maitreyi. See *La Nuit bengali.*
Mitul Reintegrării (The Myth of Reintegration). Bucharest,
1942.
Nuntâ în Cer (Marriage in Heaven). Novel. Bucharest, 1938.
Nuvele (Novellas). Madrid, 1963.
Oceanografie (Oceanography). Essays. Bucharest, 1934.
Salazar şi revoluţia în Portugalia (Salazar and the Revolution
in Portugal). Bucharest, 1942.
Şantier (Work in Progress). Indian diary, 1928–1931.
Bucharest, 1935.
Scrieri literare, morale si politice de B. P. Hasdeu (Literary,
Moral and Political Writings of B. P. Hasdeu). Edited texts,
introduction, commentaries, and bibliography. 2 vols.
Bucharest, 1937.
Soliloquii (Soliloquies). Bucharest, 1932.

La Tiganci si alte povestiri (At the Gypsies' and Other Short Stories). Bucharest, 1969. [*La Tiganci* has now been translated in *Tales of the Sacred and the Supernatural*. See above.]

Other Bibliographies

Allen, Douglas, and Doeing, Dennis. *Mircea Eliade: An Annotated Bibliography*. New York: Garland, 1980. A chronological, cross-indexed, carefully annotated bibliography.

Kitagawa, Joseph M., and Long, Charles H., eds. *Myths and Symbols: Studies in Honor of Mircea Eliade*. Chicago and London: University of Chicago Press, 1969. Contains a bibliography.

Marino, Adrian. *L'Hermeneutique de Mircea Eliade*. Paris: Gallimard, 1981.

Works Devoted to Mircea Eliade

Theses and Dissertations

Allen, Douglas. *The History of Religions and Eliade's Phenomenology*. Ph.D. dissertation, Nashville, Tennessee, 1971.

Avens, Robert. *Mircea Eliade's Conception of the Polarity "Sacred/Profane" in Archaic Religions and in Christianity*. Ph.D. dissertation, Fordham University, 1970.

Charpentier, Anne. *Sense et fonction du sacré selon Mircea Eliade*. Thèse de licence en sciences religieuses, Université Catholique de Louvain, 1975.

Deprit, Raoul. *Le Symbole chez Mircea Eliade et chez Claude Lévi-Strauss: Etude comparée*. Thèse de licence, Université Catholique de Louvain, 1975.

DiNardo, Mark A. *A Study of the Role of Symbol in the Writings of Karl Rahner, Mircea Eliade, and H. Richard Niebuhr*. Ph.D. dissertation, Catholic University of America, 1971.

Doeing, A. Dennis. *Mircea Eliade's Spiritual and Intellectual Development from 1917 to 1940*. Ph.D. dissertation, University of Ottawa, 1975.

218

Duchêne, Henri. *Le Thème du Temps dan l'œuvre de Mircea Eliade.* Thèse de doctorat, Université Catholique de Louvain, faculté de philosophie et lettres, 1965.

Dudley, Guilford. *Mircea Eliade and the Recovery of Archaic Religions: A Critical Assessment of Eliade's Vision and Method for the History of Religions.* Ph.D. dissertation, University of Pennsylvania, 1972.

Franssen, Jean. *Notion et fonction du mythe selon Mircea Eliade.* Thèse de licence en sciences religieuses, Université Catholique de Louvain, 1975.

Greenberg, Leonard. *Mircea Eliade's Mythology: A Descriptive Analytical Study.* M.A. Thesis, McGill University, Montreal, 1977.

Kraay, Robert Wayne. *Symbols in Paradox: A Theory of Communication Based on the Writings of Mircea Eliade.* Ph.D. dissertation, University of Iowa, 1977.

Lebrun, Raphael. *L'Homo religiosus selon Mircea Eliade.* Thèse de licence en sciences religieuses, Université Catholique de Louvain, 1974.

Saliba, John A. *The Concept of "Homo Religiosus" in the Works of Mircea Eliade: An Anthropological Evaluation for Religious Studies.* Ph.D. dissertation, Graduate School of Arts and Sciences, Catholic University of America, 1971.

Saracino, Antoinetta. *Mircea Eliade, Novelle.* Thèse de doctorat, Università di Bari, Facoltà di Lettere, 1966.

Scagno, Roberto. *Religiosità cosmica e cultura tradizionale nel pensiero di Mircea Eliade.* Tesi di Laurea, Università degli Studi di Torino, Facoltà di Lettere e Filosofia, 1973.

Schreiber, David. *The Value of History and of Jesus Christ in the Works of Mircea Eliade.* Union Theological Seminary, Richmond, Virginia, 1969.

Slater, R. George. *The Role of Myth in Religion: A Study of Mircea Eliade's Phenomenology of Religion.* University of Toronto, 1973.

Velz, Ewald. *Le Paradoxe de la Rédemption (Erlösung) ici et maintenant: En prenant comme "modèle" F. Nietzsche interprété principalement à la lumière des œuvres de Mircea Eliade.* Thèse de doctorat en philosophie, Université Catholique de Louvain, 1974.

Welbon, Guy Richard. *Mircea Eliade's Image of Man: An Anthropogeny by a Historian of Religions.* M.A. thesis, Northwestern University, 1960.

Wheeler, Carol, R.S.M. *Contrasting Modes of Archaic and Modern Consciousness according to Mircea Eliade.* M.A. thesis, Georgetown University, 1971.

Yrian, Stanley Orton. *Mircea Eliade and a "New Humanism."* Ph.D. dissertation, Brown University, 1970.

Monographs

Allen, Douglas. *Structure and Creativity in Religion: Mircea Eliade's Phenomenology and New Direction.* The Hague: Mouton, 1977.

Altizer, Thomas, J.J. *Mircea Eliade and the Dialectic of the Sacred.* Philadelphia: Westminster Press, 1963.

Bean, Wendell C., and Doty, William G. *A Mircea Eliade Reader.* New York: Harper/Colophon, 1975.

Culianu, Ioan P. *Mircea Eliade.* Assisi: Orizonti Filosofici, 1977.

Dudley, Guilford, III. *Religion on Trial: Mircea Eliade and His Critics.* Philadelphia: Temple University Press, 1977.

Kitagawa, J. K., and Long, Charles, eds. *Myths and Symbols: Studies in Honor of Mircea Eliade.* Chicago: University of Chicago Press, 1969.

Saliba, John A. *"Homo religiosus" in Mircea Eliade: An Anthropological Evaluation.* Leiden: E. J. Brill, 1976.

Tacou, C., ed. *"Mircea Eliade." Cahiers de L'Herne,* no. 33. Paris: Editions de L'Herne, 1978.

Selected Critical Studies

Ahlberg, Alf. "Mircea Eliade och de religiösa symbolerna." *Svenska Dagbladet,* 21 September 1966.

Alexandrescu, Sorin. "Mircea Eliade, scriitor: I–II." *Luceafarul* 11, nos. 10–11 (1968).

———. "Dialectica fantasticului." Introduction to Eliade's *La Tiganci si alte povestiri.* Bucharest, 1969.

———. "Nawoord: Mircea Eliade, of het fascinirende Vertellen, *De Mântuleasa Straat.*" Amsterdam, 1975.

Allen, Douglas. "Mircea Eliade's Phenomenological Analysis of Religious Experience." *Journal of Religion* 52 (1972): 170–86.

Altizer, Thomas, J.J. "Mircea Eliade and the Recovery of the Sacred." *Christian Scholar* 45 (1962): 267–89.

Alvarez de Miranda, A. "Un tratado de Historia de las Religiones." *Cuadernos Hispanoamericanos* 61 (1955): 109–12.

Aner, Kerstin. "Mytens man." *Var Lösen,* October 1965, pp. 355–57.

Bagdanavicius, Vytautas, M.I.C. "Mircea Eliade: Zmonijos religiniu simboliu tyrinétojas." *Aidai: Ménesinis Kulturos Zurnalas* no. 3 (New York, 1969): 115–27.

Baird, Robert D. "Normative Elements in Eliade's Phenomenology of Symbolism." *Union Theological Seminary Quarterly Review* 25 (1970): 505–16.

———. "Phenomenological Understanding: Mircea Eliade." In *Category Formation and History of Religions.* The Hague: Mouton, 1972.

Bakonsky, L. "Mircea Eliade în perspectiva unei restituiri." *Steaua* 21, no. 5 (1970): 54–58.

Balota, Nicolae. "Un hermeneut al secolului XX: Mircea Eliade, explorator al mitului." In *Euphorion* (1969).

Balota, V. "Mircea Eliade si etosul cunoasterii." *Viata Româneasca* 30 (1977): 53–55.

Balu, Ion. "Mircea Eliade, prozator. Inceputurile." *Steaua* 20, no. 10 (1969): 71–78.

Bharati, A. "Ueber Eliades Yogaauffassung." *Zeitschrift für Religions- und Geistesgeschichte* 12 (1960): 176–79.

Bîrlea, Ovidiu. "Mircea Eliade." In *Istoria folcloristicei românesti.* Bucharest: Enciclop. româna, 1974.

Bologa, Valeriu. "Documente: Mircea Eliade si istoriografia medicala clujeana." *Steaua* 20, no. 12 (1969): 176–90.

Daniélou, Jean. "Témoignage sur Mircea Eliade." *Revue des Etudes roumaines* 7–8 (1961): 217–18.

Demetrio, Francisco, S.J. "Mircea Eliade: His Methodology and a Critique." In *Symbols in Comparative Religions and the Georgics.* Ateneo University Publications, no. 3. Manila, 1968.

Dudley, Guilford. "Mircea Eliade as the 'Anti-Historian' of

Religions." *Journal of the American Academy of Religion* 44 (1976): 345–59.

Florescu, N. "Mircea Eliade si literatura populara." *Iasul Literar* no. 4 (1970): 64–66.

———. "Mircea Eliade si romanul enigmaticei R." *Manuscriptum* 3 (1972): 132–40.

Frenkel, Vivianna. "Mircea Eliade ed alcuni studiosi del suo tempo." *ACME (Annali delle Facoltà di Lettere e Filosofia dell'Università degli Studi di Milano)* 28 (1975): 173–88.

Frye, Northrop. "World Enough without Time." *Hudson Review* 12 (1959): 423–31.

Gombrich, Richard. "Eliade on Buddhism." *Religious Studies* 10 (1974): 225–31.

Hamilton, Kenneth. "Homo Religiosus and Historical Faith." *Journal of Bible and Religion* 33 (1965): 213–22.

Hof, Hans. "Religionsfenomelog med budskap: Mircea Eliade." *Var Lözen,* June 1965, pp. 251–56.

Hudson, Wilson M. "Eliade's Contributions to the Study of Myth." In *Tire Shrinker to Dragster,* ed. Texas Folklore Society. Austin, Tex.: Encino Press, 1968.

Kijowski, Andrzej. "Wizja ludzkosci nieomylnej: Mircea Eliade, *Traité d'histoire des religions.*" *Twórczósc,* no. 10 (1965): 143–48.

Lillin, Andrei A. "Arhetip si mediu în nuvela: *La Tiganci* de Mircea Eliade." *Orizont* (Timisoara) 19 (1968): 46–52.

Lobet, Marcel. "Mircea Eliade et la chronique souterraine de l'humanité." *Revue générale,* April 1975, pp. 41–46.

Long, Charles. "Recent Developments in the History of Religions Field." *Divinity School News* (University of Chicago) 26 (1959): 1–12.

———. "The Significance for Modern Man of Mircea Eliade's Work." In *Cosmic Piety,* ed. Christopher Derrick. New York, 1967.

Lorint, F. E. "L'Ouverture vers la mort dans la *Forêt interdite.*" *International Journal of Rumanian Studies* 1 (1976): 101–8.

Luyster, Robert. "The Study of Myth: Two Approaches." *Journal of Bible and Religion* 34 (1966): 235–43.

Maguire, James J. "The New Look in Comparative Religion." *Perspectives* 5 (1960): 8–10.

Mairet, Philip. "The Primordial Myths: A Note on the Works of Professor Mircea Eliade." *Aryan Path* 34 (1963): 8–12.

Manolescu, Florin. "Mircea Eliade: Romanul 'experiantialist.'" *Analele Universitatii Bucuresti, Limba si Literatura romania* 18 (1969): 131–39.

Margineanu, N. "Gândirea simbolica în opera lui Mircea Eliade." *Steaua* (Cluj) 18, no. 2 (1967): 62–68.

Margul, Tadeusz. "Mircea Eliade jako teoretyk swietosci i mitu." *Euhemer* 5 (1961): 36–52.

Marino, Adrian. "Hermeneutica lui Mircea Eliade." Parts I and II. *Revista de istorie si teorie literara* 26, nos. 2 and 3 (1977).

Masui, Jacques. "Mythes et Symboles selon Mircea Eliade." *Les Cahiers du Sud,* no. 316 (1952): 478–90.

Micu, Dumitru. "Proza lui Mircea Eliade." *Limba si Literatura* 17 (1968): 95–116.

———. "Présence roumaine de Mircea Eliade." *Cahiers roumains d'études littéraires* 2 (1974): 136–39.

———. "Mircea Eliade as a Romanian Writer." *Lisuba si Literatura Româna* 26 (1977): 63–71.

Molinski, Bogdan. "Humanistyka, Religioznawstwo i Mit samotnego czlowieka Uwagi o twórezosci Mircea Eliadego." In *Sacrum, mit, historia.* Varsovie, 1970.

"Myths for Moderns." *Times Literary Supplement* (London) 10 February 1966, p. 102.

Negoitescu, I. "Mircea Eliade sau de la fantastic la oniric." *Viata Româneasca* 23 (1970): 71–77.

Noica, Constantin. "Adevaratul înteles al *Sacrului.*" *Saptamana* nos. 261, 263 (1975).

Oprea, Al. "Mircea Eliade: Tehnica epianiei si vârstele creatiei." In *Mitul "faurului aburit."* Bucharest, 1974.

Penner, Hans H. "Bedeutung und Probleme der religiösen Symbolik bei Tillich und Eliade." *Antaios* 9 (1967): 127–43.

Pernet, Henry. "Rencontre avec Mircea Eliade." *Gazette de Lausanne,* September 1961, p. 3.

Piru, Al. "Literatura fantastica." *Romania Literara* 1, nos. 1, 5, 6 (1968).